THE POCKET GUIDE TO PANTSING

HOW TO WRITE A NOVEL WITHOUT AN OUTLINE (WITH CONFIDENCE)

M.L. RONN

Published by Author Level Up LLC.

Version 4.0

Cover Design by Pixelstudio.

Cover Art © MarkStock / Depositphotos

Editing by BZ Hercules and Audrey Weinbrecht.

Beta Readers: Eliza Bulz, Jon Howard.

Special thank you to the following people on Patreon who supported this book: Zhade Barnet, Stephen Frans, Michael Guishard, Jon Howard, Beth Jackson, Megan Mong, Lynda Washington, and Etta Welk.

Some links in this book contain affiliate links. If you purchase books and services through these links, I receive a small commission at no cost to you. You are under no obligation to use these links, but thank you if you do!

For more helpful writing tips and advice, subscribe to the Author Level Up YouTube channel: www.youtube.com/authorlevelup.

CONTENTS

Introduction   vii

PANTSING BASICS

What is Pantsing and Why Should You Write   3
Without an Outline?

Myth #1: Your Stories Will Be Inferior   9

Myth #2: You're Publishing a Rough Draft   11

Myth #3: Pantsing Leads to Rabbit Holes, and   15
Rabbit Holes are Bad

Your Top Three Goals When Pantsing   19

A Story About How Powerful Pantsing Can Be   23
in Your Life

Mindset Tactics to Conquer Your Inner Critic   27
and Beat Writer's Block

BEFORE YOU WRITE: PRACTICAL CRAFT TRICKS FOR BEGINNERS AND VETERANS ALIKE

How to Improve Your Craft Quickly   47

Analogy #1: The Writer's Rule of Thirds   49

Analogy #2: Plato's Theory of Forms   53

Analogy #3: Fiction as Fabric   59

Making It Practical: Rules of Thumb to Live By   67

Plot Basics   69

Character Basics   73

Researching a Novel Without an Outline: Some   87
Practical Tips

WRITING YOUR NOVEL: HOW TO WRITE, WHAT TO WRITE, AND WHEN

What to Prepare Before You Start Your Novel	99
Editing As You Go: The Ultimate Guide to Looping/Cycling	101
"Documenting" Your Story: Why You Should Outline Your Novel as You Go	109
How to Create a Basic Reverse Outline	113
How to Create an Advanced Reverse Outline	121
0-25%: The Honeymoon Phase and the Horrible Rough Spot That Comes After	131
25-75%: When the Novel Becomes Real	139
75-100%: The Glimmer and the Mad Dash Afterward	141
Frequently Asked Questions That Come Up During the Writing Process	143
Pantsing...on Your Phone???	157
Pantsing...with Dictation???	161

AFTER YOU FINISH: PREPARING YOUR BOOK FOR PUBLICATION

The Master Loop	165
A Solid, Easy Self-Editing Workflow to Help You with Cleaner Drafts	167
Microsoft Word Macros	171
Fact-Checkers	175
Beta Readers	183
Working with Editors	187
Into the Rabbit Hole: Mining Your Stories for Data & Analytics to Help You Write the Next Book Better	189
Parting Words	199

Resources Mentioned in This Book   201
Read Next: How to Dictate a Book   203

Meet M.L. Ronn   205
More Books by M.L. Ronn   207

INTRODUCTION

In this book, I'm going to teach you how to write a novel without an outline and feel amazing doing it.

I suspect that you found this book because you discovered that outlining isn't for you. It doesn't matter how or why. What matters is that you're here, and I'm glad you are.

You're part of an exclusive club. At the time of this writing, if you perform an Amazon search for "how to write a novel without an outline," you will see exactly five books on the topic written since 2013 (including this one). *Five* books.

If you search for "how to outline a novel," you will receive hundreds of search results. My search yielded 726 books.

Outlining is king in the writing community, but that doesn't mean that *you* have to do it. Yet, the very thought of writing without an outline is enough to make many writers break into a cold sweat.

Writing without an outline has several names: discovery writing, organic writing, writing into the dark, or most famously, "pantsing" (because you write by the seat of your pants). Learning this writing method is an eye-opening and crazy adventure. Not everyone who attempts it is successful, but those who are successful are forever changed by it.

The biggest problem with learning how to write without an outline is that there's no structure (which is ironic if you think about it). Everyone does it differently, and most writers learn in isolation. Because outlining is the common wisdom, writers may not share what they learn for fear of being looked down upon, or for fear that no one will be interested. The result is that many pantsers keep their knowledge to themselves. However, if you talk to them, the tips they share will blow your mind and change your views on how to be a writer.

Writing without an outline is like solving a Rubik's cube with no idea how to maneuver it. You can twist the cube in endless configurations and feel like you're never getting anywhere. "Pantsing" is like that; it seems impossible at first, but there's actually a system you can follow to find the solution. Like solving a Rubik's cube, it requires you to think differently.

This book covers my approach to "pantsing," and the lessons I've learned in writing over 20 science fiction & fantasy novels without an outline since 2016.

MY UNLIKELY PANTSING STORY

The year was 2015. I was an avid outliner at the time, but I was frustrated with how much time I was spending on outlining. I had written several novels and had grown increasingly tired of the outlining process.

I decided to track how much time I spent in every phase of my then series-in-progress, down to the very minute.

The time I spent looked like this:

- 20 percent outlining
- 60 percent writing the first draft

- 20 percent revising the first draft

From this breakdown, 60 percent of my time for this entire series was spent writing. The other 40 percent was not spent writing at all. Even worse, most of my emotional struggles with the novel were during the 40 percent.

Want to know the worst part? *I didn't even follow the outlines that I wrote!* The characters led me down different paths. I spent 20 percent of my time on an outline (which felt like an eternity), only to not follow it. Why was I outlining again?

I told myself that I'd rather reduce my time spent on outlining and revising, even if it meant spending a little more time writing the book.

Right around this time is when I found a guide called *Writing into the Dark* by Dean Wesley Smith. It was the answer I needed.

Dean wrote things in that book that I had never heard anyone say. He covered how to write a novel without an outline while still creating a book that readers would love. He shared tips that professional writers follow. Reading the book was like taking the red pill in *The Matrix*.

I was always taught that pantsing was a dirty word, that it was something only hack writers did. I was wrong. So much about pantsing resonated with my personality, and for the first time, I realized it was okay to embrace me and ditch outlining.

Writing into the Dark changed everything for me. My word counts exploded overnight (they were already pretty high) and my books sold better. Most importantly, writing was fun again. I gained a confidence in myself and my writing that is difficult to describe.

I have been writing into the dark ever since, and I consider myself highly versed in the method. This book details my approach to Dean's method, with some twists and lessons I have learned over the years.

Also, I would recommend that you buy Dean's book—this book will make a lot more sense if you do. This book reinforces many of the concepts he teaches, plus a few more things I've discovered.

This book will get *extremely* into the weeds of writing into the dark and pantsing. It gets into the weeds because *you're* going to be in the weeds when writing without an outline. You will need all the help you can get, and you will need it from someone who has dealt with almost every problem that comes up.

My goal is for this book to guide you during the writing process, much like *Writing into the Dark* did for me. It'll be there for you when things go wrong—and trust me, they will. Most importantly, it will illuminate the process so that you never touch another outline again.

WHY I'M QUALIFIED TO WRITE THIS BOOK

I'm the author of over 60 science fiction and fantasy novels and self-help guides for writers. At the time of this writing, over 30 of my books are novels, and I wrote 23 of them without an outline.

I also write unconventionally. I have learned to be insanely productive by writing on my phone. Because I have a crazy lifestyle, I write novels in the backseat of Uber cars, while waiting at the doctor's office, and in the checkout line at the grocery store. I also dictate, speaking my stories while staring at a wall, with no idea what's going to happen next. For fun, I once dictated an entire novel while I rode an exercise bike—into the dark!

So I write on my computer, on my phone, and I dictate my

stories, frequently switching back-and-forth between these methods...all without an outline. I've trained myself to achieve effortless pantsing.

I also run the popular YouTube channel for writers, "Author Level Up" which, at the time of this writing, has over 35,000 subscribers and over one million lifetime views. Every minute of every day, someone is watching one of my videos on YouTube. I've done several videos on writing without an outline, and my YouTube community *loves* pantsing. I get questions on it weekly.

You'll never guess what my most popular video of all time is —"How to Outline Your Novel!" Ironically, I outlined eight novels before I switched to pantsing, so I understand both schools of thought.

I've also spoken about writing to crowds of over 1,000 people: 20 Books Vegas and multiple *Writer's Digest* conferences. I've also been a featured guest on major writing shows such as "The Creative Penn."

I built my writing career while working a demanding career in insurance, raising a family, and attending law school classes in the evenings. I write five to ten books per year, sometimes more. I'm not a full-time writer yet, but I'm working pretty hard to get there.

Anyway, that's enough about me.

OVERVIEW OF THIS BOOK

This book will walk you through everything you need to know to write a novel without an outline, with confidence.

Pantsing Basics covers the basics of pantsing, myths, and your top goals when writing without an outline. If you've already committed to pantsing and don't need to learn why you should, you can skip this section.

Mindset Tactics covers how to overcome mental struggles writers have when pantsing, especially during their first run without an outline.

The **Practical Craft Tricks** section addresses one of the most common questions from pantsers: "How will I know *how* to write if I am new to the craft?" This section will answer that question and give you some useful shortcuts.

Researching a Novel will teach you how to adapt your research methods for pantsing.

Writing a Novel will hold your hand through the entire writing process. You will learn what to write, why, and when to write it. You'll also learn how to conquer writer's block. I also answer the most frequently asked questions that writers have during pantsing. Within this section, **Editing as You Go** will teach you how to edit your work while you're still writing it. **Documenting Your Story** will teach you how to outline your novel *while* you write it. (Yes, I said outline. But this is a different type of outline.)

After You Finish will discuss how to self-edit your work and how to send a clean manuscript to your editor in record time.

Into the Rabbit Hole will cover some very advanced topics that you may find insightful.

And finally, the **Resources** section will collect all the resources I mention throughout the book in one easy place for your convenience.

Also, there are a hefty amount of images in this book. I've created a place where you can view the images in high resolution in case they don't show up on your device well. View them at www.authorlevelup.com/pantsingimages.

Congratulations on embarking on an amazing journey. Pantsing is an exercise in patience, self-awareness, faith in oneself, and faith in story. I believe you'll be pleasantly surprised at what you can do after you read this book. I can't guarantee it will be easy, but I will arm you with the tools you need to be successful.

Writing without an outline is best done with the help of a guide. Let this book be that for you.

—M.L. Ronn
Des Moines, Iowa
August 25, 2021

PANTSING BASICS

WHAT IS PANTSING AND WHY SHOULD YOU WRITE WITHOUT AN OUTLINE?

Let's talk about common myths about pantsing. These are criticisms and excuses that people make about why writers can't or shouldn't write without an outline. I hope to show you that they're not true—at least, they don't have to be.

First, let's define some terms for mutual understanding.

"Pantsing" is the act of writing a novel without an outline. A "pantser" is someone who writes this way (compared to a "plotter," who is an outliner). "Writing into the dark" is also the act of writing a novel without an outline, but it is a very specific methodology. However, I will use both terms interchangeably.

When pantsing, you trade your outline for your intuition. An outline helps you know what to write next; since a pantser doesn't have one, they must feel their way through a story. Pantsers have an intuitive sense of story, which sharpens the more they write this way.

Pantsers' intuition comes from their "creative voice," a term coined by Dean Wesley Smith. The creative voice is your inner writer. Contrast that with your "critical voice," which is your inner critic. Pantsers learn to *amplify* the sound of their creative voice and *minimize* the influence of their critical voice on their work.

You might be a pantser if:

- You despise outlining.
- You outline, but the method doesn't "click" with you.
- You outline, yet find yourself straying from your outlines often, if you use them at all.
- You're a rule breaker.
- You write your stories in a nonlinear fashion. You have no problem thinking or writing out of sequence.
- The thought of writing without an outline doesn't scare you and you're willing to try it (most people have a visceral reaction).
- You want to tell stories faster.
- You prefer writing over non-writing activities like outlining and revising.

Not all pantsers are created equal. Each writes in their own personal way. However, it is useful to divide pantsers along two lines.

First, we can separate them based on how frequently they do it:

- **Serious Pantsers**: they prefer pantsing as their main writing method, but they may also still outline.
- **Ride-or-Die Pantsers**: pantsing is their *only* method of writing and they will never outline again unless special circumstances require it.

We can also divide pantsers by whether they rewrite:

- **Rewriters** believe in rewriting their work to make it better. They often write sloppy first drafts, believing they can be fixed later. They write their books in multiple drafts.
- **Anti-Rewriters** hate rewriting almost as much as outlining and will avoid it at all costs. These writers finish their books in one draft.

Please know that pantsing is not technically synonymous with writing in one draft. However, I am a Ride-or-Die Pantser and a fervent Anti-Rewriter. This book reflects those views. The authors of other books on the market skew differently. I share that so you know upfront where my sympathies lie. If you're pro-rewriting, for example, I'd stop reading and find another book to help you.

WHY WRITE WITHOUT AN OUTLINE?

Because, if you're reading this, *you* can't write any other way. Pantsing is in your DNA; you're just now discovering it.

More practically, writing without an outline is satisfying for readers if done correctly. To paraphrase an author on Quora, if you can't surprise yourself, then you can't surprise your readers.

If you can surprise and delight your readers and keep them turning the page, you'll make more money as a writer.

If you don't like outlining, pantsing will also keep your writing fun, which will improve your happiness as a writer. You'll be happier if you don't have to do it anymore.

Happy writers write better books, and better books mean

happier readers. Happier readers mean more sales because they'll readily buy everything you write.

Finally, experienced pantsers find that the method helps them write faster and more efficiently. This is because they understand story and can write clean, compelling novels with much less time and effort. These writers become crazy prolific and they write more books in *one year* than some writers will write in their lifetimes.

That said, are there cons to pantsing? Sure.

Steven James, author of *Story Trumps Structure* (another excellent book on this topic), lays out the most balanced and honest description I've ever read of the pros and cons of pantsing versus outlining. These aren't true of everyone, but I've found that they are accurate for me:

- Outlining strengths: story escalates well, resulting in great climaxes
- Outlining weaknesses: the scenes aren't always believable and the story can feel contrived
- Pantsing strengths: strong continuity and believable events
- Pantsing weaknesses: stories can wander, ramble, and be anticlimactic

These are general thoughts and don't apply to everyone.

When I was outlining, I struggled with continuity. Directionally, my stories were fine, but I had to work hard at the transitions between scenes.

When I switched to pantsing, readers said one of my stories was anticlimactic (but it still sold pretty well). That criticism resonated with me. That said, anticlimacticism and a wandering story are not always bad things, but is it possible that new pantsers could commit those sins? Sure. However, I believe they are valid criticisms that can be easily addressed by applying the principles in this book.

There is nothing inherently wrong with any writing method. The key is to understand your method's strengths and weaknesses and overlay those with your own.

MYTH #1: YOUR STORIES WILL BE INFERIOR

The biggest criticism of the pantsing method is that it produces inferior stories. After all, if you outline, you'll know exactly what happens in the story. The argument goes that, if you create a competent outline, you'll have a strong story structure, strong character development, and everything will flow in accordance with common writing craft methods.

No story I ever outlined had a perfect structure or character development, even though I certainly tried. And even if it were possible to create the "perfect" outline, that had nothing to do with how I executed it on the page.

A writing method is just a writing method. You can put a value judgment on it, but that doesn't change it. There have been hugely successful, well-respected, household name writers from *both* schools.

Also, while writers love to adhere to a particular writing structure, readers don't care so much. When readers browse for books, they don't think, "Gosh, I want to read a book written in the Hero's Journey today." They buy based on character, and if there's something off with the story, they will unconsciously put the book down. Outline or no outline, writing is about execution, and that's the only thing readers care about.

And remember that if you treat writing as a professional endeavor, you're going to use editors (and possibly beta readers) to help you catch anything glaringly wrong with your plot or characters. Editing is the great neutralizer in this debate. At the end of the day, if you do the best editorial job you can and it produces a book that readers love, what does it matter how you wrote the book? (Keep reading for more ugly myths around editing.)

All readers care about is the story. My experience is that *writers* care about structure and plot methods way more than readers do.

MYTH #2: YOU'RE PUBLISHING A ROUGH DRAFT

This myth is usually leveled at Anti-Rewriters.

"How can you actually write a good book in one draft?"

Rewriters use pantsing as a way to get the story down, then revise it until they're happy with it.

Anti-Rewriters *do* write their book in one draft.

But let's define "one draft" because it doesn't mean what you think it means.

Writers who can sit down and write perfect prose from start to finish are rare. Most writers do some level of revision—even Anti-Rewriters.

If you follow the writing into the dark method, for example, there's the act of cycling (also known as looping). In it, you write 500 words, cycle through (revise) those words, write the next 500 words, then rinse and repeat. You will also revisit many sections to make minor corrections throughout the drafting process, usually because you will write something later in the book that impacts what came earlier.

Cycling is really just editing as you go. To argue that pantsing produces unedited books is not an accurate portrayal of writing into the dark, or serious pantsing, for that matter.

Technically, if you write into the dark, you're writing multiple drafts, but you're doing it strategically. When you write "The End," you will have gone over the entire novel several times, each time making corrections here and there. If you added up all the changes, they would probably be substantial. So, if you do the method correctly, it will produce a finished manuscript that is *not* a rough draft.

Is it possible that some writers do blaze through their novels, have no sense of their ability, and hand their work to an editor, leaving the editor to pick up the pieces (or worse, self-publish that work without editing)? Yes, I'm sure that happens all the time, but that's not what professional writers do. That's why this argument is a myth.

No Outline = More Revision. Also a Myth.

That insidious statement is a variation on this myth, and it puts droves of people off pantsing forever.

"You do realize that if you write without outlines that you will have to spend more time in revision, right?" is what people (usually outliners) say to pantsers. Some pantsers believe it.

In the previous section, I explained how the "pantsing = rough draft" argument is a myth.

Some people presume that if a book is not written with an outline, that it will eventually have to be brought into accordance with *some* story structure.

Why?

As I said before, readers don't care about structure; they care about execution.

Story structures are just suggestions, and something someone made up. There are grains of truth in many, but to implement them wholesale will probably make your story wooden.

Also, how do you know that following a story structure will guarantee reader satisfaction? Just because a *writer* thinks a problem exists in a story doesn't mean the *reader* will care. If you don't believe me, pick any novel off your shelf and chart its structure. I bet you could find structural issues or items that need additional work. Yet, it probably sells quite well despite that.

Structure is just a suggestion. If you follow the advice in this book, your stories *will* have a structure. You'll do it subconsciously because you've probably already internalized the structures that resonate most with you. I'm amazed at how closely my novels align with certain story structures, even though I don't think about them. It just happens.

But next comes another common question: "How does one learn structure if they *don't* at least outline a novel or two prior?" After all, it's hard to understand story structure until you've built a story for yourself.

Framing it as a chicken or egg question is a legitimate concern. Do you need outlining experience to understand story? In other words, should writers "graduate" into pantsing?

I certainly did, but I don't think it's a requirement. I didn't plan it that way. I will admit that understanding certain outlining methods has been helpful for me, but that doesn't mean that writers *have* to outline first. But if you want to pick up some craft books on it, I don't think there's anything wrong with that.

Focus on the methods in this book, write the best stories you can, and commit to writing and reading a lot. You'll find that story structure will not be a problem for you.

MYTH #3: PANTSING LEADS TO RABBIT HOLES, AND RABBIT HOLES ARE BAD

Another common myth is that pantsing leads to rabbit holes, and that rabbit holes are bad.

Pantsing is also known as discovery writing. You're exploring your story and discovering what to write as you go. Occasionally, you will discover that you went down a dead end, and you'll have to backtrack and go down a different path. This is part of the process. That's why it's called *discovery* writing. When you fly by the seat of your pants, sometimes your pants will rip! That's okay.

If you're scared of dead ends, this writing method just isn't for you. Sorry.

I encounter rabbit holes all the time. In my last novel, I had my hero talk to his neighbor, and I *thought* the neighbor was going to play a role in the story. Halfway through the novel, the story took me away from that possibility, so I had to go back and cut that chapter. It was around 1,500 words. I threw them all in the trash. Some would view it as wasted writing, but I didn't. I shrugged and kept writing.

That scares some writers, but you can't have your cake and eat it too. Writing into the dark means...well, you're in the dark and you're going to have to feel your way around. That's why pantsing is about trusting your intuition.

But you might be thinking, "If that's true, why did your intuition lead you to a dead end in the first place?"

Let's return to the concept of your creative voice. Your creative voice is like a mouse in a labyrinth when you write without an outline. It smells cheese and it is trying to find it. Occasionally, it makes a wrong turn. But the mouse always finds the cheese. Your mind is the same way when telling a story; it'll find the cheese if you dare to listen, be patient, and do what your creative voice tells you. That's a hard concept for beginners to understand, but it'll make sense in time.

I can't tell you how many times I think "No, that won't work" when my creative voice makes me write something, only to go "wow" near the end of the novel because it knew what it was doing all along.

This is why rabbit holes aren't bad. If you're not willing to venture where your creative voice sends you, you won't unlock the true benefits of pantsing.

"But, Michael, you're telling me I have to throw away words from time to time? Isn't that inefficient?"

Not really. Cutting words is still more efficient than rewriting. You cut them and then you move on.

I've written over 20 novels with this method, and the most I've ever thrown away was about 5,000 words. Most novels, I don't throw anything out. If I do, it's usually a few hundred words.

If you find yourself throwing out huge chunks of words, then keep learning the craft and possibly look within to see if other factors are driving it, such as self-doubt.

Let's talk about the root cause of why this myth scares so many people: uncertainty. When writing without an outline, you must learn to live with uncertainty. For the most part, you have no idea what will happen in the story. That's unnerving to many people. Most prefer stability and security. If that's you and you're not willing to change that, then this book won't help you in your writing career.

However, if you can learn to live with uncertainty and the unknown, magical things will happen if you let them. And the hard truth is that some of those magical things just happen to be inside rabbit holes.

YOUR TOP THREE GOALS WHEN PANTSING

Now that we've defined pantsing and dispelled some of the surrounding myths, let's talk about strategy.

You have three goals when writing your novel without an outline:

1. To write well.
2. To write cleanly.
3. To write efficiently.

To write well, we have to be students of the craft and keep practicing. I offer some tips about how to improve your craft later in this book. Writing well is about writing with emotional resonance, clarity, and skill. It's about executing all the writing elements beautifully on the page (character, action, dialogue, and so on).

To write cleanly, we have to commit to getting the story right the first time. If an issue comes up, it means stopping and fixing it immediately. Sloppy writing is our biggest enemy—it's easy to do, but if you resist its siren call, you'll save yourself hours of time and effort.

It's easier to fix plot problems while they're fresh in your mind. You'll solve them better that way too. Otherwise, if you let problems sit, they will breed, and you'll have more problems to address later. As a rule of thumb, fix problems *now* or they'll double.

I'll teach you how to avoid writing sloppily. It just requires you to be vigilant and proactive, that's all. You'll be shocked at how much time you'll save, which leads to the third goal.

To write efficiently, we have to rethink how we approach the page and adjust accordingly.

Let's look at the definition of "efficient" in Merriam-Webster:

"productive of desired effects; especially: capable of producing desired results with little or no waste (as of time or materials)."

Writing efficiently means producing a well-written, clean, finished novel in as little time as possible, with little waste.

If my definition of efficiency resonated with you, then you will understand why I dislike multiple drafts and rewriting.

The more efficiently you can tell a good story, the sooner you can share it with the world, and the sooner you can start writing your next story. While other people are stuck in outlining or revision hell, you'll be writing and having fun.

In the introduction of this book, I explained how I wrote a series where 20 percent of my time was spent outlining, 60 percent writing, and 20 percent revising. When I began pantsing, the distributions changed. Now, I spend approximately 90 percent of my time writing and 10 percent revising (as I go). I spend zero time outlining (beforehand) or rewriting, and, as a result, I write my stories faster.

Do I have some waste? Yes, as I mentioned in the previous chapter. But it's not that much compared to when I was outlining and rewriting. Not even close.

Efficiency is not on the minds of most writers, but it should be. It's how you become prolific.

If you're committed to writing well, cleanly, and efficiently, keep reading.

A STORY ABOUT HOW POWERFUL PANTSING CAN BE IN YOUR LIFE

Before we continue, I want to share an idea from *Writing into the Dark* that changed everything for me, and hopefully, it will for you too.

In the book, Dean Wesley Smith writes: "...Writing into the Dark takes a belief system in story. It takes a trust that your creative voice knows what it is doing. And it takes a vast amount of mental fight [...to] let the fine work your creative voice has done alone and not ruin it with your critical voice."

Writing as a belief system.

After I read that quote, it got me thinking about my relationship with religion.

I believe in a higher power. I can't prove it, though. For example, I could tell you about an emotional experience I had that gave me faith, but you can't see it. I can't really convince you that a God exists.

Yet I still choose to have my own belief system because of faith.

Faith is believing in something even if you can't see it, even if you can't prove it. Without faith, you don't have a belief system. It's the cornerstone on which any belief in ANYTHING intangible rests.

I'm going to get philosophical for a minute, but writing for me is a sacred act. It's as sacred as prayer.

When I sit down and write and simply trust my creative voice and have full faith in it, I'm connecting with something higher than myself, for reasons beyond myself.

Because I don't outline, I never know where my story is going to go, but I trust my creative voice. And it always, always, always comes through for me. It has never failed me. Not once.

But that, like belief in any major religion, takes an incredible amount of faith. And I'm not a religious person.

Let me tell you another story.

When I decided to put writing into the dark into action, I tried it with *Old Dark*, Book 1 in my *Last Dragon Lord* dark fantasy series. (Side note: I wrote my book *Old Dark* in the dark. Get it? Haha...)

I wrote this book with no outline, no idea of what was going to happen except an image of the first scene in my head. The story is one of the most interesting, twisting narratives I've ever written.

It's the story of Old Dark, a supreme Dragon Lord who has ruled the world for hundreds of years with brutality. He's a supervillain. When an assassination attempt on his life goes wrong, he falls asleep and wakes up 1,000 years in the future, in a society ruled by his enemies.

The story starts in *A Game of Thrones*-like, high fantasy world, but as I explored it, it morphed into a futuristic urban fantasy as you follow Dark on his quest to seek revenge and reclaim power. It has a lot of plot twists, a lot of players, politics, and is quite Shakespearean in tone. In other words, it's the kind of book most writers would try to outline first because it's pretty complex.

When I published the book, readers said some interesting things in their reviews. They were posting things like the story was deliciously good, it kept them wanting more, and all kinds of other things that I had never seen them write before.

That was when I knew that I was onto something.

So let me bring this full circle for you: I was frustrated with outlining and committed to stopping doing it. I followed the writing into the dark method, wrote an entire series without an outline, and readers praised me for it and didn't even know the difference. And ultimately, my story and characters were better for it. All of that because I trusted my creative voice to do its job.

If that's not a success story, I don't know what is.

If you've never done this before, trust me: I know it's hard to give up the safety of outlining and venturing into the dark instead.

To use Dean's analogy from the book, it's like journeying into a dark cave without knowing where the exit is. It's pitch dark, and you can't see anything, not even your hand in front of your face.

It's scary too. You fear what you can't see, and everything is new and frightening. There are creepy stalagmites and stalactites, hidden bodies of water, and at every turn, it seems like you run into a dead end. A few times, you want to quit and run out of the cave and back into safety.

If you remain patient and push through the discomfort, you'll eventually find the exit. And when you emerge on the other side, it'll be one of the most amazing things you've ever seen: fearlessness, self-confidence in your writing, satisfied readers, and a better story—all converging into the incredible euphoria of a finished novel. Anything feels possible.

You'll have so much more confidence and feel so much better about yourself and your writing that it won't even be funny.

But to get there, you've got to get through the cave. And the first time around, I'm not gonna lie—it's a bitch. But it gets easier every time you do it as long as you have faith and trust your creative voice.

That's why you should read *Writing into the Dark*, and why it was such a transformative book for me.

But I'm done selling you the virtues of writing without an outline. It's time to get to work.

MINDSET TACTICS TO CONQUER YOUR INNER CRITIC AND BEAT WRITER'S BLOCK

This chapter is about mindset, but I'm not going to go woo-woo on you. Instead, I'm going to keep it practical (because we have to be efficient, remember?). I'm going to give you several tools you can use to cultivate a winning mindset and conquer your inner critic.

Your biggest foe when writing without an outline is uncertainty.

What is uncertainty? According to Merriam-Webster, it's *"the quality or state of being uncertain: DOUBT."*

When you are uncertain, you are more susceptible to self-doubt and second-guessing. This is because uncertainty carries risk: your story could bomb, readers might leave you bad reviews, and you'll have wasted time, effort, and money on a book that doesn't sell.

To be clear, writing a book with an outline carries the same level of risk, but it doesn't feel that way because outliners *feel* in control. But let's be honest—plotters write books that fail too.

If you want to be successful at this method, then you *must* learn to live with uncertainty. Notice that I didn't say "eliminate" uncertainty. That's not possible. But you can learn to coexist with uncertainty.

Let's talk about some critical tools you need to navigate the mental struggle.

A SIMPLE EQUATION FOR SUCCESS

Remember this equation: consistency + curiosity + tenacity = success.

$$Consistency + Curiosity + Tenacity = SUCCESS!$$

View in high resolution at
www.authorlevelup.com/pantsingimages

You can become a successful pantser by practicing a **consistent writing habit**. Write every day if you can, but if you can't, write as much as your schedule and personal life permit. The more you write, the better you will become. This is because you'll encounter new story situations you've never dealt with before. As you solve them, you'll develop muscle memory.

How many words should you write per day? As many as you can without getting sloppy. If you can, I recommend a daily minimum. At the time of this writing, my daily minimum is 2,000 words per day (and 1,000 words on Sunday). I often write much more than that, but by setting a daily minimum, I keep my writing skills sharp.

You don't want your writing skills to go dull. Trust me when

I say there's nothing worse than leaving a novel halfway through and picking it up again several months or years later. Not only do you have to remember what you wrote, but you also have to sharpen your craft skills again. This is why professional musicians practice their instruments every day without fail—missing one day makes them feel rusty. You too should write as frequently as possible to avoid this problem.

To become a successful pantser, you must also develop **curiosity**. Never get complacent. There's always something new to learn, and you should keep experimenting. Every writing session is an opportunity to try a new skill. Every writing session contains a scenario that you've never handled before. Relish those experiences. If you do, you'll keep your writing fun, and when you're having fun, you'll write better.

For example, in a recent novel, I told the story from the third-person limited point of view. I floated in and out of several characters' heads. I came to a scene where one of the supporting characters was telling my heroine a sad story. The character telling the story was not one of the viewpoint characters.

What I could have done was write a wall of text and use vivid language and an interesting hook to keep the reader turning the page. Instead, I wondered what would happen if I tried something unusual.

When the character started telling his story, I switched to the first-person point of view (POV). His story goes for about 1,000 words before reverting to the third-person limited through the viewpoint of the heroine who was listening to him. It's the only time in the series that I do this.

Boy, did I break a bunch of rules...but I followed my curiosity. Will it work? I don't know, but it made for a unique writing session, that's for sure. If it fails and readers call it out, I'll know why. If it succeeds, though...well, isn't that fascinating? Developing a curiosity mindset will pay off dividends for you over the long term.

To become a successful pantser, you must also cultivate **tenacity**. If you've never written without an outline before, the first time will be *hard*. You'll question everything you ever knew as a writer. The fear is so powerful, it makes people quit, especially new writers. It takes tenacity to keep sitting down in the chair when your critical voice and self-doubt keep kicking your ass. It takes true courage to listen to your creative voice—it's a whisper that is difficult to hear at first because your critical voice is screaming at you. Eventually, you'll learn what your creative voice sounds like and you'll be able to tune out the critical voice's anger.

Oh, and guess what? The closer you get to finishing your novel, the angrier your critical voice will get. It will throw everything at you to make you quit—and I mean everything.

The good news is that when you finish your first novel without an outline, the next one will be much, much easier. That's not much consolation, though, when you're in the middle of your novel and you hit your first rough spot.

Like I said, tenacity.

Remember: consistency + curiosity + tenacity = success.

Consistency
+
Curiosity   = SUCCESS!
+
Tenacity

View in high resolution at
www.authorlevelup.com/pantsingimages

If you write consistently, you will eventually emerge from any rough spots you encounter.

If you cultivate curiosity, you'll delight your readers (and yourself) during your writing sessions, which will make for more interesting stories.

If you practice tenacity, nothing will be able to stop you.

LET'S TALK ABOUT FEAR

I've mentioned fear many times so far in this book. Let's talk about what it really is.

Merriam-Webster defines fear as *"an unpleasant often strong emotion caused by anticipation or awareness of danger."*

Whenever I think about fear, I think about a lecture by Gavin de Becker. De Becker was Oprah Winfrey's chief security consultant, and at the time of this writing, he works for Jeff Bezos. His job is to protect ultra-wealthy people. He wrote a book called *The Gift of Fear* that explores the biology of fear and how it can save our lives.

In his lecture, de Becker discussed how fear is a biological response that we evolved to protect us from danger. In prehistoric times, if a human walked past a bush, something could have been hiding in it, waiting to kill them. Thus, fear was justified in that circumstance because it kept our ancestors alive.

De Becker tells a story about a man who was swimming and suddenly was attacked by a shark. His fight-or-flight instinct kicked in as he lay tangled in the shark's jaws. For some reason, he took his fingers and jammed them into the shark's eyes. The shark went wild and dove toward the ocean floor. Against all reason, the man held on. Eventually, it let him go, and he swam to the surface. That act of holding on ultimately may have saved his life because he blinded the shark and it lost so much energy, it probably couldn't have attacked him again if it wanted to.

In that story, fear saved that man's life. He experienced a biological response that kicked in to save him. This is why de Becker's book is called *The Gift of Fear*.

What does this have to do with writing? For starters, when you sit down at the keyboard and suffer from a nasty bout of writer's block, the emotions are pretty damn similar to the fear of getting eaten by a shark (at least they were for me when I started writing!).

However, the fear you experience when you stare at the blinking cursor or when you imagine readers hating your work or some other thing you're worried about is not *fear*. It might feel like fear, and it might sound like fear, but it's not. It's *anxiety*. There's a difference.

Hell, even the definition of anxiety in Merriam-Webster is similar to fear's. Note the words I've bolded: *"apprehensive uneasiness or nervousness usually over **an impending or anticipated ill**: a state of being anxious."*

Fear: *"an unpleasant often strong emotion caused by **anticipation** or awareness of danger."*

Both fear and anxiety are similar in that they are a response that forms in *anticipation* of something dangerous. In the case of fear, it's a shark that is currently turning you into a meal, a sabretooth tiger popping out of a bush, or a burglar holding a gun to your head. In the case of anxiety, it's writer's block.

De Becker's message is to stop being afraid of the things *you imagine*.

I'm going to make a radical prediction: the next time you sit down and can't figure out what to write, a sabretooth tiger is not going to burst through your window and devour you. Whatever you're afraid of probably won't come to pass.

If a sabretooth tiger does interrupt your next writing session, you have my permission to tell the world I'm full of crap (if you live to tell about it). Until then, be free and don't let anxiety win.

If you understand and internalize this advice, then your critical voice won't be able to control you anymore. Anxiety is the critical voice's best tool.

Reduce your anxiety around writing and you will have a fighting chance to coexist with the presence of uncertainty.

LET'S TALK ABOUT WRITER'S BLOCK

Every writer deals with writer's block, but it hits pantsers especially badly. At least outliners have an outline they can refer to. You have nothing.

As we'll discuss many times in this book, you will have moments where you get stuck. That's okay and part of the process.

In my book, *Be a Writing Machine*, I discuss how to beat writer's block forever. It's surprisingly simple: you must uncover the root cause of the block.

Writer's block has three root causes:

1. Fear
2. Lack of inspiration
3. Personal circumstances

We talked about fear. Read *Be a Writing Machine* for more strategies to fight it. I also wrote another book called *The Indie Author Bestiary* that also deals with battling fear and other common writing monsters.

If the root cause of your writer's block is fear, then you must confront it head-on. That means sitting in the chair and grinding and following some of the other strategies I lay out in my other books.

Lack of inspiration is about filling your creative well. Developing a consistent reading habit, watching movies, exposing yourself to new people and places regularly, and being adventurous in life will fill your creative well so that it doesn't run dry when you're writing. Also, using a note-taking app like Evernote or Microsoft OneNote to capture ideas as they come to you is a smart investment in preventing writer's block in the long term. (You can use a physical notebook to capture ideas too.)

I'm especially fond of a method promoted by Claudia Azula Altucher in her book *Become an Idea Machine*. It's called idea sex. It's when you combine all of your ideas into a single place and browse through them. They start to merge into each other and become new ideas. When I encounter a rough spot, I can refer to the thousands of ideas I've captured over the years. I usually find something interesting to use as a jumping-off point.

If your well runs dry when writing, do something new. That usually will kick-start your creative voice.

In a recent writing session, I wasn't sure what to write, and I stared at the blinking cursor for a few minutes. I decided to stop writing for a while so I could mow my lawn. I listened to a podcast, and it was an interview about politics. One of the speakers said something that sparked an idea for my novel (that had nothing to do with politics). As soon as I finished the lawn, I had the best writing session of the week, writing several thousand words in just one sitting. All because I listened to my creative voice and filled the well.

Next, let's talk about personal circumstances. Life happens. We get sick, our loved ones get sick, we go through tough times, or busy seasons at work. Sometimes other obligations call us away from writing for a time. Your creative voice won't let you write if there is something important you need to deal with. It's a defense mechanism. Sometimes, it's not safe to write.

For example, my basement flooded a few years ago. Late at night, I was lying in bed, writing a book on my phone, when I heard a loud crash in my basement. Thinking it was an intruder, I ran out of bed and hurried downstairs.

It was a mop. It fell because a torrent of water flowed out of my sewer and knocked it over. My basement was covered in two inches of black, disgusting water.

Do you think I got any writing done the rest of that night or the next morning? Nope.

I didn't have any time to write for the next week because I was dealing with the water mitigation people, the insurance company, and contractors for repairs. It took a week for me to sit down at my computer, and when I did, I had a staring contest with the blinking cursor. I didn't know why because I had taken care of the issue for the most part. Still, my creative voice wouldn't let me write. Turns out, the next morning, I had a confrontation with the contractor that delayed my repairs. I don't know for sure, but I think my subconscious knew that was coming. If my creative voice let me write, I probably would have let my guard down because the book would have been floating around in my head while I was dealing with the problem— sometimes I can be scattered when I'm racing to the end of a book.

But guess what happened as soon as I resolved the conflict with the contractor? I was back to writing again like nothing had ever happened.

My personal circumstance story was relatively benign, but I have plenty of them. Life will take you away from writing for a time, and sometimes life sucks. Sometimes you have to grieve. Other times, you just don't have the mental bandwidth to write. It's okay to not be okay. Take time off, handle the problems you need to handle, and you'll find that when you do, the writing will be there for you.

Those are the three root causes of writer's block. Your job is to identify which root cause is creating the current block.

View in high resolution at
www.authorlevelup.com/pantsingimages

Use this chapter as a rule of thumb to determine how to attack your writer's block. Do this and you'll find that it goes away faster.

BEWARE STORY VISIBILITY PROBLEMS

Another problem you will encounter regularly is a unique phenomenon that I call "story visibility." No one prepared me for this, so I want to help you with it.

If you've ever flown on an airplane, you know what visibility looks like. Some days, there are no clouds and you can see the blue sky for miles. Other days, the skies are cloudy and all you can see is the underside of a giant cumulus column. Sometimes, it's storming and you're flying in blue skies over storm clouds.

Writing without an outline is similar.

Some days, you will have "clear sky" visibility: you'll know exactly what you need to be writing, and you'll even know what is supposed to come next. You might even be able to "see" in your mind how the narrative will unfold over several chapters. This is a great feeling and it makes you more confident in your writing sessions.

Some days, you will have "cloudy sky" visibility. You'll be

able to see, but not as far. You might know what you should write in your immediate chapter, but as soon as you're done with it, you might see a wall. This is when newbies start getting scared.

And finally, there is "stormy sky" visibility. You won't be able to see a damn thing in your story and the only thing you'll have to rely on is your fingers. On days like this, you just have to keep going.

Here's the great secret to pantsing: some of your best days will come from cloudy and stormy visibility days, not clear sky ones.

Understanding what kind of visibility day you're having is very, very useful.

Here is my experience:

- Clear sky days eventually give way to cloudy ones. Whenever you feel confident about what you're writing, it won't last forever.
- Clear sky days also spawn stormy skies out of nowhere. Be ready for them. Sometimes you think you know what will come next, until suddenly, you don't. This often takes new and less experienced writers off-guard.
- Stormy skies aren't as bad as they sound. The key is to keep writing, even if you're producing low word counts. No storm lasts forever. Eventually, you will write something that clears up the sky and you'll be able to see ahead again.

The next question you might be thinking is "But *why* can't I see what's next?" Go back to my section on writer's block. It's because there's a root cause. Your creative voice needs something, and it's your job to help it.

Think about this like a partnership between you and your creative voice. Your creative voice tells the story, but it needs you to keep feeding it, that's all. Visibility issues are just obstacles in the creative voice's way. For example, you might stumble into a cloudy sky visibility day because your creative voice needs inspiration. Get your inspiration, and the skies will clear.

That's why it's so important to learn how to listen for your creative voice—it's a whisper, but when you hear it, it will tell you exactly what it needs. So, put another way, you must learn to "see" what visibility you're dealing with and simultaneously listen for the creative voice to gauge what it needs. That's the best way to think about story visibility, and again, something I wish I had known when I started writing into the dark.

Keep story visibility in mind. It's a helpful tool to use along with the root causes of writer's block.

BEWARE EMOTIONAL UNDERCURRENTS

Emotional undercurrents are another phenomenon while pantsing that no one told me about when I started.

In addition to story visibility, you need to keep in touch with your feelings while you're writing.

Before you write me off as a typical millennial, consider a few things.

Our feelings interfere with our writing more than we like to acknowledge. Anything that happens in your personal life *will* affect your writing.

However, here's what I wish someone would have told me when I wrote my first book into the dark: feelings are like the weather. If you don't like them, just wait a little while.

Writing can be an emotional rollercoaster if you're uninitiated. Many types of feelings can manifest themselves in your writing sessions:

- happiness
- euphoria
- excitedness
- contentment
- "flow"
- self-doubt
- anger
- fear/anxiety
- exasperation
- sadness
- and more

Feelings are fleeting. You may experience self-doubt in a morning writing session, but later that night, you may slip into flow and write an amazing scene. The key is to understand yourself, acknowledge the feelings, and wait them out if necessary.

Recently, I went to West Palm Beach, Florida with my family. We spent a day at the beach. As we walked along the shore, the moody waves of the Atlantic Ocean rushed across our feet and beach flags flapped in the wind on a lifeguard tower.

Beach flags are interesting. They tell you how the ocean is feeling.

- Green flags mean safe waters.
- Yellow flags mean choppier currents and to swim with caution.
- Red flags mean unsafe conditions, such as rip-tides and tall waves.

Is the ocean always calm? No. It changes. If you don't like it, just come back tomorrow.

Your soul is a beach, and there are emotional undercurrents. There are rip-tides too—they always take you by surprise and they're pretty awful.

It's normal to experience many feelings as you write. No feeling is out of bounds. But feelings are also fleeting. They never stay for long. This is true of both good *and* bad feelings. Emotional undercurrents are ever-changing.

Here's another great secret of pantsing (and writing in general): your emotions and your writing quality have nothing to do with each other.

In other words, just because you're feeling bad or doubting yourself during a writing session, that doesn't mean the quality of your words is bad. It may very well be the opposite.

I experimented with one of my novels. After every chapter, I wrote down my emotional state after finishing the chapter—Great, Good, Average, Bad, and Very Bad. I wanted to see if my feelings about the manuscript correlated with the editorial process.

I hypothesized that the chapters where I felt the worst emotionally after writing would have the highest number of suggestions from my editor.

I was wrong. It turned out that chapters where I felt bad or very bad emotionally produced no more edits on average than chapters where I felt great. My mood did not correlate to the number of edits I received. This meant that *the words I wrote when I felt terrible were just fine*. Read that last sentence again and let it sink in. Talk about eye-opening!

Yet, it's easy to confuse feelings and writing quality.

The crazy thing about feelings is how suddenly they happen, and often out of nowhere. Let me tell you a few stories:

- One morning, I woke up and happened to read the news. There was an article about the 2020 US election on the front page of the site I visited. I don't know why, but I got this feeling of dread that I couldn't shake all day. It showed up in my writing session, making it hard to write. I didn't realize where the emotion came from until later that day; once I did, the feeling evaporated as soon as I identified it. Be extremely careful when reading the news!
- One day, I was talking to a friend who was going through some hard times. I empathized with him, and I found myself feeling badly throughout the day. It had nothing to do with me.
- I received a one-star review that hit me very personally. As much as I tried to ignore it, that review damaged my writing session that morning. That's why you shouldn't read reviews!
- One day, I was functioning on four hours of sleep and I had all sorts of weird thoughts while I was writing. It had nothing to do with the story, but I thought the story was crap (even though I liked it the day before!). It wasn't the story; I was just tired. If you're sleep-deprived, you're more likely to trash your writing!

I could tell you many more stories of how emotions try to sabotage your writing. So, divorce your feelings from your words. They're not related.

It is critical to ask yourself where your feelings are coming from. It's best if you can do it in the moment. Often, you'll find that you bring feelings from somewhere else into your writing sessions, but you won't realize it at first. The moment you do, the feeling will usually evaporate.

Emotional undercurrents are completely out of your control. The only thing you can do is manage them. They're an occupational hazard.

We writers are sensitive creatures. It's why we're able to do what we do, but sometimes, our emotional sensitivity is a liability.

Use this chapter as a rule of thumb when managing your emotions.

Emotional Undercurrents	What it looks like	What to do
Smooth	You feel great while writing. You enter flow.	Enjoy the ride
Choppy	You feel fine but fear is lurking nearby. Your critical voice is a quiet whisper trying to knock off your confidence	Beware your emotions
Dangerous	Your critical voice is yelling. Feelings of self-doubt	Engage in radical self-care and honesty with yourself; wait out the storm

View in high resolution at
www.authorlevelup.com/pantsingimages

Once I discovered the presence of emotional undercurrents, I became unstoppable. Now, I seldom get pulled away by an emotional rip-tide. It used to happen to me all the time, especially when I started writing into the dark.

You've no doubt felt many of the emotions I described in this chapter. Whether you agree with my advice or not, ask yourself: are you managing your emotions or are your emotions managing *you*?

I don't know a single pantser who doesn't wrestle with this. Most just don't admit it for fear of looking weak or silly. Professional writers learn to tame the struggle. Everyone deals with it in their own way.

I'm just sharing the quiet parts out loud because I wish someone had told me about it.

OTHER MINDSET TRICKS

Here are a few other tips that you may find helpful on your pantsing journey.

First, you won't remember your novels after you're finished. Whenever you encounter a rough spot, it feels like the biggest problem in the world. Once you publish your novel, you won't even remember where the rough spots were.

I agonized over my first novel back in 2013. All these years later, I look back at it and I don't even remember the sections where I had writer's block! Now I don't stress over my novels. I'm not going to remember where I had the writer's block anyway.

Second, I learned early on to let readers determine what's strong and weak about my novels. They're the only ones who matter—not an editor, your family, or other writers. Only readers matter. *Paying* readers.

You might write a scene that you think doesn't work, but maybe it's just fine in the reader's eyes.

How will you know if readers will like your story or not? You won't, unless you have the courage to publish.

Third, but what if readers *do* hate your story? Shrug and move on. Writers make novels out to be extremely important affairs, but they're just practice sessions. You're not the same writer for Book 2 as you were with Book 1. Just keep writing and commit to getting better. Developing a "practice" mindset is tough for many people because they don't want to "waste time" in their writing sessions, but trust me, you're not wasting time. More writing equals more experience, and that will help you with readers in the long term. If you write a bad book, almost no one is going to buy it anyway, so the amount of readers who *do* hate your story is likely to be pretty small. They'll probably forget your name in a few years too. You can't make any mistakes in writing that will be tattooed on your forehead for the rest of your life. (I wrote a novel with about an anthropomorphic broccoli hero, for crying out loud, and hey, I'm still here.) Many people find what I just said to be terrifying; I find it freeing because it means I can make a boatload of mistakes when no one is watching! That's the best time to learn.

Also, remember that some books gain new lives. You might write a book that doesn't sell today, but years from now, the market can change. Think about all those people who wrote vampire books before the *Twilight* series. Overnight, vampire novels were "hot" again. Every genre and subject matter has cycles of boom and bust.

And finally, if you publish a book that doesn't sell, the root cause may not be your writing. It could be your cover, your book description, your formatting, or your marketing decisions. It could also be that you were ahead of your time or that the type of book you wrote isn't popular (right now). That shouldn't stop you from continuing to write.

BRINGING IT ALL TOGETHER

You must learn to coexist with uncertainty. You do this through:

- consistency + curiosity + tenacity = success
- getting your anxiety under control (stop being afraid of things you imagine)
- arming yourself against writer's block
- understanding "story visibility"
- managing through emotional undercurrents that happen while you're writing

Follow the tips in this chapter and you'll develop the right mindset for successful pantsing.

BEFORE YOU WRITE: PRACTICAL CRAFT TRICKS FOR BEGINNERS AND VETERANS ALIKE

HOW TO IMPROVE YOUR CRAFT QUICKLY

A common question and concern with pantsing is how to learn the craft. The books on pantsing are in the single digits, but there are hundreds of outlining books. Plotters have almost unlimited writing craft resources and support.

I can't teach you how to write, but I can teach you how to think about writing. But I suspect you're not looking for a book on writing theory—you've probably read plenty already.

Theory is great, but it's useless if you can't put it into practice.

I took an online course about video editing. The instructor was a seasoned video director. He said something in the course that resonated with me. To paraphrase him (and substitute his advice with writing advice), I can teach you all about writing theory, plot, and characters, but it will mean nothing to you if you can't apply it. One of my favorite quotes from him is "I'm not an academic. I'm a pracademic."

I too am a pracademic.

You'll be able to use the advice in this chapter in your next writing session. I hope that it will give you some comfort when you're writing into the dark for the first time.

If you like the material in this section, I wrote a book called *How to Write Your First Novel* that goes into great detail on how to write your first novel with style.

ANALOGY #1: THE WRITER'S RULE OF THIRDS

I want you to think about the following framework. It will help you realize what you already know, focus on what to work on, and guide you when you get stuck. I call it the Writer's Rule of Thirds. These are rules of thumb, not prescriptions, but they'll help you manage the uncertainty.

RULE #1: YOUR BOOK HAS THREE PARTS

First, let's talk about story and the Three-Act Structure.

I guarantee you know this already.

Act One: Setup. Reader meets the hero and the stakes are introduced.

Act Two: Confrontation. The stakes rise, the hero experiences a string of successes and setbacks against the villain.

Act Three: Resolution. Tension reaches its highest level. There is a final battle with the villain, the tension is reduced, and loose ends tied up (or not).

To keep this simple, the Three-Act Structure is really just a beginning, middle, and end. Every story has a beginning, middle, and end, right?

RULE #2: EVERY CHAPTER IN YOUR BOOK HAS THREE PARTS

Just as your story has a beginning, middle, and end, so do your chapters. Every chapter has setup, conflict, and resolution. The resolution is usually a cliffhanger that makes the reader want to turn the page.

RULE #3: EVERY SECTION IN YOUR CHAPTERS HAS THREE BUILDING BLOCKS

Quick exercise: grab any contemporary commercial fiction novel and turn to a random page. On that page, three elements are working in tandem to comprise the story: dialogue, narrative, and action (let's call it DNA for short).

Dialogue consists of three parts: quotation marks, the words being said, and a tag, such as "he said." That's it.

Narrative is more expansive. For example, the narrator may be telling the reader about something, such as the background of a place, summarizing an event, or details about another character (known as exposition). When this happens too frequently, readers may accuse the writer of "telling" and not "showing." When it happens too little, readers may say that the book moved too fast or lacked character development.

Action is action: characters in movement, propelling the story forward. Action differs from narrative because it advances the story, whereas narrative slows it down.

If you think about DNA as Legos, you can snap them together to "build" your story. If you and I were to build Lego castles, yours would look different from mine, but the building blocks would be the same. Stories are the same way. Every writer builds their stories differently, but the underlying blocks are the same. This is why you can open up a Stephen King novel and see pages and pages of narrative, or a James Patterson novel, where you'll see a mix of all three elements—switching almost like clockwork—or a Nora Roberts novel, where dialogue is the star, especially when the romance is growing.

There is no right or wrong way. Just your way.

We could also talk about point of view, pacing, character development, and other elements of story that you've no doubt heard of, but really, those elements are dependent on how you put your DNA together.

Just remember the Writer's Rule of Thirds: your book has three parts, every chapter in your book has three parts, and every section in your chapter has three elements: dialogue, narrative, and action.

Understand that framework, and suddenly, your story ideas will have a dependable, reliable structure that you can follow from start to finish, especially when you're stuck on cloudy and stormy visibility days. If you're staring at the blinking cursor, ask yourself where you are in the chapter—beginning, middle, or end? How might that help you figure out what needs to come next?

Remembering the DNA analogy is also helpful because you'll remember that every chapter is just dialogue, narrative, and action. Snap those Legos together and pretty soon you'll have a castle.

ANALOGY #2: PLATO'S THEORY OF FORMS

The following excerpt is from my book, *Mental Models for Writers*. A mental model is a framework you can use to change your thinking so you can solve a problem. In it, I discuss Plato's Theory of Forms. Yes, there is some philosophy in it, but I make it practical at the end. I'm including it because it will help you see the craft differently, and it will increase your awareness of what it takes to improve your craft.

———

We turn to the world of philosophy, with the famed Greek philosopher, Plato, as our guide.

Plato posed many ideas and theories that shaped western civilization, but the one that impacted me the most when I read his work was the theory of the forms.

I promise to keep this practical and easy to understand, but stick with me, even though it may get a little weird at times. I can't promise to any philosophers reading this that I'll get my interpretation of Plato 100 percent correct (few do), but bear with me.

Plato concerned himself with *big* things like justice, virtue, and good, what they look like, and how society achieves them. He used the theory of the forms to explain what "vague" concepts like virtue and justice might be, and to do this, he used an example most commonly referred to as "chairness."

What is a chair?

It's a thing we sit on, to be sure, but what is it, really?

Craftspeople all over the world can make chairs, but each one would be different. One person's chair might be made of wood, another of plush, another of metal. One might have wheels, one might have arms, and others still might have unique purposes, such as a barber's chair or a director's chair. Yet, all of these are still chairs, and at their core, they have a fundamental essence that makes them chairs, and not, say, desks. This essence is known as "chairness."

The funny thing about chairness is that craftspeople all over the world create chairs independently of each other—two people who don't know each other could theoretically create almost identical chairs.

Plato theorized that we have in our minds a dim vision of a "form" of things—in other words, an exact, perfect image of what a chair should look like. But it's not truly *in* our minds—it exists in another world that we lived in before we entered this one, and this other world has perfect "forms" of every thing that ever was. Plato argued that the world of the forms is reality and our existence is just a replication of it. Our world is ever-changing and deteriorating—after all, even the best chairs don't last forever—but the world of the forms is perfect and unchanging.

Forms are the ideal, and Plato believed that the pursuit of these forms could teach us how to live better.

In the case of the chair, there's a perfect form of a chair in the world of the forms, and all of our chairs in this world are an imperfect execution of that form.

WHAT IS A STORY, CHARACTER, OR SETTING?

We can apply Plato's theory of the forms to writing.

Have you ever wondered how two writers who don't know each other, who live in two completely different parts of the world can come up with almost identical story ideas?

What if it were true that fiction "forms" existed, and every writer in history was just trying to recreate them? What if different writers saw the same forms but from a different angle, depending on their upbringing and life circumstances, which might explain why we have such diversity in fiction?

We might call these different fiction forms "storyness," "characterness," or "dialogueness."

If writers are in fact recreating imperfect forms of a perfect mental image, how does skill level factor into the equation? What is the difference between a mega-bestseller like Stephen King and an amateur who has no understanding of fiction and who writes terrible prose? It might be true that the difference between these two writers is that Stephen King has developed a "clearer" line of sight to the world of the forms, thus allowing him to execute at a higher level. Not perfect, but more perfect than the beginner. Therefore, if that were true, then the best advice to the beginner would be to learn how to "see" what he or she cannot see, and to go on a Pokémon quest of sorts to collect as many forms as possible to learn how to write better fiction. The beginner would learn to see new elements in the writings of bestsellers and figure out how to recreate those elements in their own work.

I recognize that this argument is reductive, and it doesn't take into consideration environment, luck, personal connections, right time, right place, and so on, but isn't it intriguing to think that writers all over the world and throughout the ages are connected by one common thing—our connection to the forms? If it were true, it would be an incredibly special relationship, one that only a small percentage of the population experiences. If we took this further, it could lead us down the path to discover what "writerness" is—our very essence as writers and as human beings who have chosen to express ourselves through the written word.

MAKING IT PRACTICAL

Consider that every fiction technique has a corresponding "form"—in other words, a perfect execution that will keep readers hooked every time.

Every writer is simply trying to "see" the form so that they can execute it the same way. But no execution is perfect. Some are better than others, though.

Take the example of backstory. How do you do it? This is a commonly debated fiction technique. Everyone agrees that backstory is important, but some writers seem to misuse it. Worse, readers can't agree on how they like to see it.

If I were to ask myself the question, "How do I write an effective backstory that engages the reader while also enhancing the story?", I would have to embark on a journey to discover what the "form" looks like.

I would read as many books as possible and observe how each writer does it, how readers respond, and most importantly, how *I* respond as a reader. Every example I read would help me build a mental image of what the form might look like. I might find that, rather than existing as a flat image, the form might be multidimensional, and that the vision I see depends on where I'm standing. For example, I might need to use a different technique for science fiction versus historical fiction, or a different approach for a hero versus an antihero, to use very simple examples. But once I could get a line of sight to the form, I would practice replicating it whenever I needed to write backstory, with varying degrees of success until I could finally find a combination that works for readers.

Such a journey could take me a few days or decades, depending on how clear my initial line of sight is.

That's just one form. There are hundreds if not thousands more. That may sound overwhelming, but mastering writing means mastering as many forms as possible. Not even the mega-bestsellers can master them all. But if you can master, say, ten to twenty forms and be intentional about them, that's probably more than 80 percent of the writing population, and readers will notice.

<hr />

From now on, when you read a novel, start collecting forms and pay attention to how authors execute them. Write down your observations. Collect forms and commit to experimenting with them in your next writing sessions.

But how do you *study* another writer, you might ask? Turn the page.

ANALOGY #3: FICTION AS FABRIC

First, let's start with a helpful analogy that will help you see fiction differently.

In *Mental Models for Writers*, I talk about an unusual paradigm shift I had about the craft of fiction. It's called "Fiction as Fabric." It pairs very nicely with Plato's Theory of Forms and it will teach you how to study other writers. Here's what I wrote:

———

There's an outlet mall near my city that people like to visit because it sells name-brand clothes for cheap. The mall has a reputation for low prices, but it also has a notorious reputation for defective clothes if you aren't careful—a designer shirt with the seams in the wrong place, for example. Once, I bought a button-down Oxford shirt with a crooked sleeve—I won't make that mistake again.

Whenever I shop at this outlet mall, I've learned to check the seams on every item I buy. I inspect every item carefully, running my fingers along the seams and checking the handiwork. I turn the item inside out and then check it again. I buy the item only when I am certain that it doesn't have any defects.

One time, I was shopping and found some great shirts after inspecting them carefully. My wife was still shopping, so I followed her around while she looked for clothes. I pulled out my phone and started reading a Michael Crichton book. Around this time, I considered myself a virtual student of his, reading through his entire bibliography and learning the exact techniques he used to keep readers enthralled.

Standing in an ocean of clothes racks and trying to study a Crichton technique, I made a strange connection—when I looked at his writing, I saw "seams." Patterns that I never saw before were blinking at me on the page.

Take an early chapter of *Jurassic Park*. It begins in Costa Rica, in a village hospital in the middle of a rainstorm. A construction crew rushes in a victim who has been hurt in a construction "accident" (read: dinosaur attack).

The first few hundred words of the chapter are about the rainstorm and how powerful it is, and the backstory of the doctor who has traveled to Costa Rica from the States as a visiting physician. Then the story proper begins as she hears a helicopter in the rain.

Here's the pattern that immediately jumped out at me:

* Establishment of the setting and character's backstory of why they are there
    * Turn of thought
    * Action
    * Turn of thought
    * Section break
    * Action
    * Viewpoint character observing another character
    * Turn of thought

Could you detect the seams? They're the turns of thought (which I will explain). Crichton couches his techniques between them.

The best way to see this is to look at the written page.

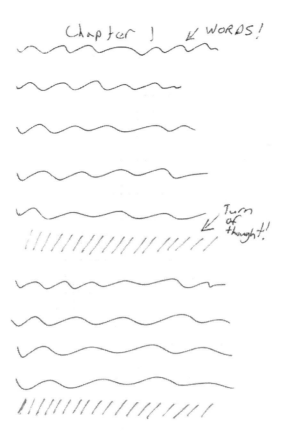

View in high resolution at
www.authorlevelup.com/pantsingimages

Let's go through it again with a little more detail.

His establishment of the setting and the character's backstory is one self-contained technique. There's a certain way that he does it.

The first turn of thought is an observation the character has about the setting that serves as a trailing off before she hears the helicopter in the rain. The turn of thought serves as a transition from her thoughts back into the action.

The next section has almost no narrative; it's action and dialogue as the helicopter flies through the vicious rainstorm and struggles to land on the helicopter pad. It's a symphony of sensory detail, followed by another turn of thought, which is the helicopter crew calling for a doctor.

Then we have a section break, followed by a standard scene with the doctor interacting with the crew as she treats the accident victim.

Crichton does this over and over again consistently throughout the book. Mastering the "turn of thought" is a technique that will take you one step closer to writing on the level of the mega-bestsellers because they are connectors. To master turns of thought, you simply have to be aware of them and see the many different ways they can be done.

If you want to write like a master, couch your writing techniques between seams.

I've found that whenever I read a section of Crichton's that makes a big impact on me as a reader, all I have to do is look between the seams, and I can easily break down how he did it.

And this isn't special to Crichton. Virtually *all* of the mega-bestsellers do this—Stephen King, John Grisham, Nora Roberts, James Rollins, James Patterson, and J.K. Rowling, for example. Take your pick of any top writer and examine their handiwork, and you'll see the "seams." It's one of the few easily distinguishable marks of mega-bestselling fiction.

I can't emphasize to you enough that discovering this was a

watershed moment for me. As my fellow millennials would say, I was shook.

When you see this for the first time, you will never un-see it.

If you understand fiction as fabric, you can use this mental model in three ways:

* To analyze bestseller craft techniques in isolation so that you can understand how their techniques kept you engaged as a reader

* To be more cognizant of the "seams" in your own writing so you can be intentional about them

* To elevate your writing to the next level

Let's take a quick detour for a moment to the land of writing education because I want to dispel a few myths.

How exactly do you study the craft of writing? Most writers find the process overwhelming because there's little structure. If you go to a college class, the professor will usually have you analyze an entire work, break it down into its core parts, and put it back together again. The result is that students usually learn nothing about the craft itself. University writing classes are almost always story-focused and word-focused. They emphasize story at its highest level (through workshops) but also writing good sentences. There's almost no emphasis on actual technique, which I call "the missing middle."

As a professional fiction writer, I've had to throw out what I learned in school and replace it with a more practical way of studying fiction.

My advice: do not study entire books. If you sit down and try to read every page for wisdom, you'll walk away frustrated and you'll learn nothing.

Instead, study the techniques that made an impact on you when you read the book the first time as a reader. If a technique resonated with you, then you should incorporate it into your toolbox. Study those tools and study them in isolation.

For example, there's a sequence during the final battle of *The Andromeda Strain* by Michael Crichton that is a super-advanced way of "head-hopping" between two viewpoint characters. He doesn't do this anywhere else in the book, and if you're not paying attention, you'll miss it. When I read it for the first time, I thought, "Wow! How did he do that? He violated a commonly accepted rule of fiction."

I studied how Crichton did the head-hopping—nothing more, nothing less. I looked for the seams first, and sure enough, he did it cleanly—the jump from one character's head to another is so clean and smooth that most people probably missed it. And the *way* he did it was super high-class.

If I wanted to use this same technique in my own work, I know exactly how I would do it based on looking at Crichton's seams. I would simply sew the section in a similar way.

If I *really* wanted to, I could take this even further and integrate Plato's theory of the forms model. I could "collect" literary techniques that I find interesting and I catalog them to use later; maybe I'd remember that John Grisham did this in a novel too, and then I can compare his and Crichton's technique for "head-hopping-ness," the fundamental commonality that both authors share when implementing this extremely advanced fiction technique. I would form a mental image in my head of what perfect head-hopping *could* look like, and I would use that as my mental model when executing it.

Anyway, I've taken this detour to illustrate that studying fiction works best when you study elements in isolation. It sounds counterintuitive, but it works.

To bring this full circle, you probably don't think about the seams of your clothes when you put them on in the morning. Readers don't see the seams in the books they read either.

Everything I've just told you in this chapter is invisible to them; they never, ever see it.

The goal is for your readers to *never* see or think about the seams in your work. If they do, you're doing it wrong.

You don't want your book to look like the defective shirt at the outlet mall. You want it to be that comfy t-shirt that the readers feel at home in and never want to take off.

This skill, unfortunately, can take a lifetime to master. But you can start using it today, in your next writing session.

MAKING IT PRACTICAL: RULES OF THUMB TO LIVE BY

I've given you some analogies to think about in this chapter, but let's bring them together.

The Writer's Rule of Thirds teaches us to think in thirds: divide our story into thirds, divide our chapters into thirds, and divide our sentences into three elements: dialogue, narrative, and action. This is a helpful compass when we get stuck.

Plato's Theory of Forms teaches us that there are writing "forms" out there. The mega-bestsellers are masters of these forms, and we can see these forms most clearly by studying their work. If we do, we'll improve our craft faster.

Fiction as Fabric teaches us that the best way to study mega-bestsellers is to look for the seams. The "forms" we seek are between the seams. If we want to improve our craft with real, practical results, we can study writing techniques in isolation so that we can figure out how they wowed readers. Then we can use those same techniques in our work. This helps us add pizzazz and spice to our writing sessions, and it also keeps them fun.

To the question, "How do I improve my craft," that's the

answer. Of course, reading writing books, taking courses from professional writers, and continuing to write consistently will help you improve too. It's not hard, but it's not easy. It's simple.

PLOT BASICS

Let's talk about plot. It's easy to overcomplicate plot, but I'm not going to do that. I'll keep it simple by giving you some basic rules of thumb.

The best plot structure that "clicked" with me is the plot point theory. Syd Field wrote about it in his book *Screenplay* and Larry Brooks popularized it for writers with his book *Story Engineering*.

The premise behind the plot point theory is that every plot has a series of events that propel the story forward. These events are universal, and you can best see them at work in movies (for example, every Pixar movie follows this method like clockwork).

The *inciting incident* puts the story into motion.

The *first plot point* is the point of no return, when the hero makes a choice that puts them on the road to fight the villain. This point is like a door being shut behind the hero. This is usually around the 25 percent mark.

The *first pinch point* is an encounter with the villain that sets the hero back, though it need not be the first encounter with the villain.

The *second plot point*, or *midpoint* is when the hero goes from reactive to proactive. They often realize an important detail that will help them beat the villain. This is around the 50 percent mark.

The *second pinch point* is another setback from the villain.

The *third plot point* is the calm before the storm when the hero readies themselves to fight the villain. This is usually around the 75 percent mark.

The *black moment* is the low point when all seems lost. The hero needs help. This plot point can also appear before the third plot point.

The *final battle* is the face-off against the villain.

The *resolution* is the ending, when most or all loose ends are tied up.

Of course, there are many variations. For example, a book can have many pinch points—not just two. But the basic structure is pretty useful.

The plot point method is great for beginners because it's easy to understand and you can observe it in many modern movies. The problem with the method is that it is quite formulaic, so beware of that. Also, it doesn't help you with character development. It only covers plot.

I am not suggesting that you follow this method. I'm sharing it so that you can be aware of it because you'll find that your story will probably contain many of these plot points.

If you write your story trying to hit the plot points, you've missed the message of this book. Instead, think of these plot points as potential indicators of where you are in the story so you can get a sense of where your creative voice might be headed.

I find that every story I write usually hits the plot points. It happens without me knowing about it. But sometimes it's useful to know what plot point might be coming up next, especially when you're stuck.

For example, the midpoint is generally when the hero goes from being reactive to proactive. There's usually a moment or a piece of information that helps them make the transition. If you're in the murky middle and your hero hasn't made the transition yet, then maybe that's where your creative voice is going. There might be something the character did in a previous chapter that leads to this transition. You just have to look for it. Let your creative voice lead the way.

This is a useful trick when you're in a stormy visibility day. Just don't let it derail your creativity.

I learned a lot of outlining techniques, trust me. The plot point theory is the *only* one that manifests itself continuously in my writing, novel after novel. Maybe it will be true for you too.

CHARACTER BASICS

Let's talk about characters. So much character advice is theoretical, but I want to give you some advice you can use on the page.

CHARACTERS MUST HAVE THE ABILITY TO CARE

Years ago, I was super happy when I stumbled upon the book *Creating Characters: How to Build Story People* by Dwight V. Swain. He is most famous for his book *Techniques of the Selling Writer*, and you may have heard of it, but I believe *Creating Characters* is a much better book.

The reason I like it is because when I read it, it validated many things that I'd experienced in my career that I already knew to be true.

I won't cover everything in Swain's book because you should read it, but the main premise of the book is that the key element that every hero must have is the ability to care. Not goals, not flaws, but something they care about.

Swain uses the analogy of a newlywed husband and wife.

The husband is a clean-freak and very orderly. To his surprise, the wife isn't. Of course, that bothers the husband because he can't stand messes, which creates conflict.

The ability to care is what Swain calls the "dominant dynamic," and it's what fuels the character. It's more than a goal to achieve something—it's more fundamental than that. And I argue that it's something that you probably already know about your character before you do any of your prep work.

RATIONALIZING THE CHARACTER

We've talked about the foundation of a character, which is the dominant dynamic. The next brick in the pyramid, so to speak, is what Swain calls rationalization.

Rationalization is the process that the WRITER follows to create depth to the character by giving them actions and emotions. It's the heart of what writers do.

To do it, though, requires the real-world skill of being a student of people.

Let's say that I'm writing a main character who is impatient. I need to find ways to make that apparent and memorable.

In real life, the place where I work has a restroom with lousy automatic soap dispensers. Half the time, they don't work, and when they do, they give you so little soap that you have to get two servings to even wash your hands.

Once, I saw an executive stand at the middle sink and stick his hands out to both soap dispensers on the right and left sinks so he could get two pumps at the same time. It's an interesting gesture that an impatient person would do.

As a writer, rationalization begins when I take an element from someone I see in the real world—the executive at the sink—and I impart that element into a character.

Why did the executive do that at the sink?

I have no idea, though it's probably because the sinks are lousy. But I don't know for sure. Maybe he was late to a meeting, or maybe it's just a weird personality quirk.

In real life, people don't want to be rationalized. Do you think it would have gone well if I'd asked the executive why he used two soap dispensers at the same time? No. People generally don't want to have to explain why they do what they do or why they feel what they feel. It's exhausting. Sometimes they just don't know why.

But in writing, that's where the true magic is. As a writer, you don't have to know the real-life reason, but you get to invent a compelling reason why a character would do it.

If I were to have my character do the exact thing at a sink in my novel, I would first show the character doing it as descriptively as possible, like, "Standing at both sinks, I put a hand under each soap dispenser and waited for the carefully measured buzzes of soap." Then I might have the character comment on how he hates this bathroom because the soap dispensers are pathetic. He should be out catching a killer, but instead, he's playing handsy with a soap dispenser that doesn't love him back. In just a sentence or two, I've rationalized the character's actions.

I've given the reader an insight into the character through their action and opinions, and if I've done my job, readers will both see and connect with that. They might think, "I do that too!" or "That's a genius idea," or "Wow, this guy needs to calm down."

Regardless, I've forced them to look inward and start rationalizing themselves. When you do that, you create a connection.

Good writers are experts in rationalizing characters, and it's an essential skill if you want to write well.

REAL CHARACTERS ARE SUBJECT TO THE LAWS OF PSYCHOLOGY

Anyway, back to the book. Swain talks about rationalization in the book over and over, because it's important.

When you rationalize the character, you make them more memorable, but you also make them feel real.

This brings us to the golden idea of the book: **To write an amazing main character that readers don't forget, you as the writer have to pretend the character is real.**

You have to make the character appear as if they actually exist, that they are someone that the reader could see themselves meeting. You do that through careful details. Now, personally, Michael La Ronn's opinion only is that rationalization is best done when it happens in real-time when you're writing. You can't really plan it. I liken it to sketching. Sure, you have an idea in your head about what you want to draw, but when your pencil hits the page, it doesn't quite turn out like you planned. Sometimes you draw something else.

When you are writing your character, be open to where the process can lead you, and don't be afraid to borrow and steal things you've seen in real life. You'll find that it makes for more engaging fiction.

So how do we make this practical when we show up to the page?

A consistent theme throughout the book is that psychology is also an important area to learn because if you understand the psychology of real people, then you can use that skillfully with your characters. Remember, you have to treat the character as if they were real.

Think about the last friend you made. Within seconds of

seeing them for the first time, you formed a first impression, right? Right, wrong, or indifferent, you labeled them based on everything that has happened in your life up to that point. That person can either confirm your belief or subvert it.

It's the same thing with a main character. You give the reader a first impression, and you do that through the use of character tags, which could be anything from mannerisms, a certain pet phrase, a favorite hat or jacket, or the way they see the world. Water those tags in like you'd water seeds into dirt, using them a couple of times to help the reader see it.

Give the reader that first impression, and once you've done that, and if it's interesting, the reader will keep reading and spend more time with that character.

Think about that friend again. When you met them, you formed your first impression. But then you started to spend more time with them, and you started to get a sense of who they were, right? You noticed the qualities that made you want to be their friend. You became intrigued by them.

When this happens, you move from the first impression to what Swain calls a "dominant impression," which has four components: sex, age, vocation, and manner.

Swain uses the example in the book of a "loud, pushy, middle-aged female travel agent." This tells us quite a bit about the character and colors our opinion of her.

Let's break down the four components of a dominant impression, which I think would be better to call a second impression.

Sex and age are pretty self-explanatory. A character's vocation is what they do, usually their profession. This is universally important no matter what genre you're writing in. It's critical to establish this early because it's usually central to the plot. Through their vocation, you learn their manner, which is a fancy way of describing what they're like. For example, if the main character is a photographer, how is she with her clients in the first chapter? Is she sarcastic? Relatable? Pushy because she has another photo shoot in twenty minutes?

The important thing to remember about dominant impressions is that, just like in a friendship that you strike with someone, you don't start telling them your whole life story on day one. That's creepy. You do it slowly over a couple of weeks or months. With a character, you do this over a series of a few chapters, and you do it through the character's appearance, actions, dialogues, back story, and opinions. At this point, readers have a deeper impression of the character.

And herein lies another problem with writing that you need to be careful of: disengaging readers from your story.

BEWARE OF DISENGAGING READERS

You've done the hard work of knowing the character's core and rationalizing the character, but certain pitfalls can pull readers out of the story, according to Swain. Seven, specifically.

Number one is falling out of viewpoint, like accidentally switching points of view to another character, which is disorienting to the reader because they're in your main character's head. Usually, this is an editorial issue, and there IS a way to do this in a way that doesn't disengage readers, but that's beyond the scope of this book.

Number two is failing to do enough research. If you're writing a police officer, and the character does things that a police officer would never do, readers will bow out of the story. (I have some advice on how to avoid this later in the book.)

Number three is telling instead of showing. D'oh.

Number four is failing to suspend the reader's disbelief.

Number five is failing to foreshadow and springing things on the reader without a good reason to do so.

Number six is distasteful acts, like rape, incest, child molestation, senseless killing, or other things that society at large finds reprehensible. This, of course, depends on the genre, but generally, most people don't want to see your main character raping someone, even if they're an antihero. Don't do it.

Number seven is a worldview that contradicts the readers' view of the world. If, for example, the main character is anti-Muslim, that's going to disengage a lot of people, and it would take a lot of skill and grace to write a character like that in a way that doesn't turn off the majority of your readers. It's less about being politically correct than it is about remembering that your readers are an extremely diverse group with many backgrounds.

Avoid those seven things and you'll protect your character work and ensure that readers will keep reading your story.

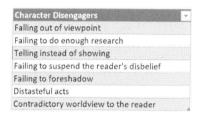

View in high resolution at
www.authorlevelup.com/pantsingimages

PUTTING THIS INTO PRACTICE ON THE PAGE

I have covered a lot so far. Let's recap.

* The core element of any character is the ability to care about something. To make the character come alive, you "rationalize" them by taking elements from people in real life and imparting them into your character. This helps readers connect with them because, ultimately, readers want to read about a character that

FEELS real, so you've got to pretend that the character is real when you're writing.

    * Give the reader a first impression of your character, followed by a dominant or second impression that explains the hero's age, sex, vocation, and manner.

    * Avoid disengaging readers by following a few common-sense tactics when you're writing your story.

I hope you can see why I like Swain's book, and I haven't even scratched the surface of other really important topics he covers.

TAKING IT A STEP FURTHER: CHARACTER DEVELOPMENT

How do you develop a character? How do you develop your hero so that readers identify with him or her?

    What about character arcs, emotional arcs, round characters, flat characters, foils, and all the other things they taught you in school?

    Throw them out the window.

    Yes, I'm telling you to throw out character arcs along with all the other stuff.

    Why?

    At this moment, someone somewhere is probably cursing my name and poking a voodoo doll with my face on it.

    Let me explain.

    The standard way writers are taught character development is to create a character arc. There are many character arc methods out there, but the one thing they have in common is that they require you to develop your arc *before* you start writing. There are various "character sheets" you can fill out to help you with this.

    This method often recommends that your character should

have *this*, you should make the reader feel *that*, have your character progress to the point of X by the 75 percent mark...

I believe that this advice is irrelevant and not practical in a real-world novel BEFORE you start writing.

Here's why. Think back to the example I gave of character manners.

If I were to attend a cocktail party, would it be appropriate for me to make a list of people that would be attending, then decide *before I even met them* how I wanted to make them feel about me? Would it be appropriate to try to engineer their response?

I don't know about you, but that would be pretty disingenuous and downright manipulative.

If you wouldn't do this in real life, why would you do it with a character?

I know, I know—I'm drawing comparisons between fiction and reality, but readers don't see the line between the two. By the very nature of writing fiction, you're asking them to suspend their disbelief.

Your hero might as well be a real person to readers. Look at the reviews of any bestselling book and you'll see that readers identify with the characters, not the plot. They laugh and cry with your characters.

So...if you treat your characters like mere characters and not larger-than-life figures that readers expect them to be, then you're probably going to swing and miss.

And if you try to engineer a character that pushes readers' buttons at just the right times...well, I argue that it's going to come across flat.

Just as you wouldn't pre-engineer people's emotions in real life, you shouldn't do it with your characters. That's why I believe that mapping out character arcs before writing adds no value to the writing process.

Here's the secret I learned the hard way while pantsing: character development happens on the page, in real-time, as you write.

This applies to virtually any character you write, not just the hero. You can and should develop supporting and minor characters too—just not as thoroughly.

I challenge you to think about character development differently.

I challenge you to change your understanding, broaden your perspective, and narrow your focus.

CHANGE YOUR UNDERSTANDING

Character development is not:

* deciding how readers should feel. Only they decide that.
    * deciding how your character should feel. Only they decide that.
    * detailed emotional and psychological arcs before writing.

BROADEN YOUR PERSPECTIVE

Most writers I know think of character arcs as a series of events. The character does this, does that...

I need you to broaden your perspective.

Character development is:

* The character interacting with settings and other characters, and how the character responds to those interactions.
    * The reader experiencing those settings and other characters, and forming their opinions about the story.

* The area between the hero's response and the reader's opinion.

In my day job, I used to be a manager. Everyone in our department wants to be promoted and they always ask what they can do to get to the next level. Most of the time, they want a checklist of things they can *do*. And trust me, there's no shortage of things they can *do* to prepare themselves for their next opportunity.

But here's the problem: you can have two equal people that *do* the same things, but the person that gets promoted is often the one who uses those experiences to develop themselves.

In other words, just because someone *does* something like attend a conference or obtain a mentor doesn't mean that they will be promoted. How they *respond* to new events and experiences is *how* they develop, not the mere fact that they did them. What ultimately matters is how they use those experiences as a starting point to think differently and improve their work product, professionalism, or contacts.

I challenge you to broaden your perspective. Instead of having a character simply *do* things, can you instead think about what those "things" *do* to the character? How does the character respond and feel? That's the essence of how people in real life grow and develop.

NARROW YOUR FOCUS

Character development is:

* The reader experiencing the struggles right alongside the character in real-time, through solid sensory details.
    * Dialogue (internal and external) of the character.
    * Narrative told through the perspective of the character.

* Actions of the character on the page.

In other words, character development is DNA...

You can map this stuff out all day long, but what ultimately matters is how you execute it on the page.

And sorry, I don't care how adept an outliner you are. You can't outline DNA.

So what that you planned to have the character caress a puppy in the sixteenth chapter? Do you execute on it from a DNA perspective? Does the reader respect the character as a result of what you've written?

We all plan novels with the best of intentions. But remember that outlines change...

Throughout a story, characters change, even if you make plans...

Instead, listen to the character. Find ways to develop them on the page through DNA. Don't refer to fancy character arcs, because readers don't gauge a story based on its arc. When was the last time you heard a reader say, "I love this story because every point on the hero's character arc was painstakingly mapped out?" Not very often.

Instead, you hear stories of how the character felt real or felt like someone the reader knew. That kind of emotional impact doesn't happen through planning out an arc.

It happens through writing, listening to your instinct, and focusing on what's on the page. It's the "micro moments" that readers remember.

For example, I love Alex Cross novels by James Patterson.

In *Along Came a Spider*, there is a fantastic sequence of scenes where Alex Cross visits Miami to pay a ransom to a serial killer. In just a couple of chapters, you learn an incredible amount of information about Alex:

* While going for a quick swim at the hotel, he muses through narrative about how he always exercises anywhere he goes.

    * He connects with the book's love interest, Jezzie Flanagan, who happens to be swimming at the same time as him. Over a few scenes, they have a sexual encounter, but not before Alex muses about the societal views on a black man sleeping with a white woman.

    * The next day, Alex visits Disney World to pay the ransom. The payoff goes wrong, and he is taken hostage on a small plane traveling God-knows-where, with a mysterious man who takes the money and runs, leaving Alex to think quickly about how to escape. Except...he's handcuffed to a seat.

In just a few chapters, I identified with Alex in more ways than I can count.

The character development that ensues is not the fact that he does the things he does, but how he responds. The mental back-and-forth he has with Jezzie Flanagan is fantastic. The actions he takes in the scenes during the payoff show what a good cop and quick thinker he is.

Does Alex mature throughout these chapters? No. But Patterson helps me meet Alex where he is.

You too should help your readers meet your character where he or she is. You can't know where your character is until they're on the page.

If you want to review your character's development *after* you've written the story, that's better. But review the DNA by enhancing what's already there—not through a graph, chart, or formula of what someone "thinks" your hero should be. And don't rewrite!

As I look back on my early novels, the most time I wasted was in plotting character development.

Readers never respond the way you think they will. They will surprise you.

Don't force your character development. Let it be organic, and remember that the key is in your DNA.

Follow the advice in this chapter and you'll write engaging characters, even if you don't know what their arcs are or how they're going to develop throughout your story.

RESEARCHING A NOVEL WITHOUT AN OUTLINE: SOME PRACTICAL TIPS

I often receive research questions when pantsing.

Research is important whether you outline or write without one. Most novels need some level of research—some more than others.

First, *should* you research before writing if you're pantsing?

Second, how should you research?

Remember our three goals when writing:

1. To write well
2. To write cleanly
3. To write efficiently

Research is important because if you don't get certain details right, readers will either stop reading or they'll call you out on it.

Research can certainly help us write well, but it is primarily an issue of efficiency.

Research tends to paralyze writers because they don't know when to stop. There are books, blogs, and podcasts that recommend extensive research templates, with world-building checklists that are sometimes many pages long.

That's garbage. And woefully inefficient.

Here's what you need to know: there are two types of research that you can do. Follow the advice in this chapter and you will become a more efficient writer with research that helps your readers stay spellbound.

METHOD #1: FOUNDATIONAL RESEARCH

This is the research you need to do before you can even start writing.

For example, if you want to write a Regency romance, but you know nothing about England during the British Regency, you would need to spend some time understanding how people spoke, how they dressed, what everyday life was like, and so on. Otherwise, you'll write a novel with incorrect factual and historical details.

If you want to write a hardboiled detective novel that takes place in your hometown, that might be easier. Assuming you don't need to do much research on your town, you would just need to make sure you're getting the police procedure right.

If you want to write a science fiction novel about artificial intelligence, you would need to read up on current theories and philosophies about the future of artificial intelligence so that your technology is plausible.

However, the research you need to do is only what arms you to write the first chapter of your book. No more.

Here's what most writers do: they surf the Internet, go to the library, interview people, read all the books in their genre, buy nonfiction books on the topic, listen to podcasts on the topic, and scour any resource they can to learn about the potential world they want to create.

Any of those topics by themselves are fine, but where writers go wrong is that they believe that they need to do them all.

I know writers who spend months researching. If that's you, then you're doing it wrong (unless you're writing in a genre that requires extensive research, like historical fiction or very hard science fiction).

I had to do a significant amount of foundational research for my science fiction series, *Android X*. It takes place in the year 2300, where androids and humans live together in peace after a devastating singularity. During my foundational research, I had to understand the following areas before I could start writing:

- Artificial intelligence: How it works, projections from experts on what it would look like in one hundred to two hundred years. In other words, what do scientists think androids will be able to do, and are there limits?
- Futurism: How would I project the future so that it feels plausible?
- World governments: My story involves a universal world government, so how could something like that happen and exist in my story without readers rolling their eyes?
- Technology: What kind of technology would exist in the year 2300 and how would it shape people's everyday lives?

These items were what I needed to write a convincing and compelling first chapter. Nothing more, nothing less.

Foundational research is like a gate. If the gate is closed, you can't go through it. But once it's open, you can proceed. Fortunately for you, the gate always opens sooner than you think. It opens once you have enough to write the first chapter.

The key is knowing when the gate opens. Many writers only need to know a little bit to begin their journey, yet they keep researching, even though the gate is wide open and swinging in the wind.

For my *Android X* series, I did three simple things that helped me create a plausible futuristic world and characters in less than two weeks.

1. I read two layperson-centric books by experts: *Physics of the Future* by Michio Kaku and *Think Like a Futurist* by Cecily Sommers. I read them simply to understand the broader concepts of what two experts in their fields think about the next couple hundred years. I kept the focus of my novel within the philosophical constraints of these two books. This way, I didn't have to worry about doing too much additional research and it gave the technology and society a cohesive theme. (It also helped that I agreed with their viewpoints.)
2. I watched an hour's worth of relevant YouTube videos.
3. I found a long-form blog post on a magazine website that explored virtual reality.

After that, the gate opened.

It's true that I still didn't understand all the intricate details I would have needed to know. It's also true that I still had research left to do.

But the foundational research helped me understand the basics so I could get started. In the reviews for *Android Paradox*,

Book 1 in my *Android X* series, readers said they enjoyed the futuristic setting. Very few quibbled with the science.

That's what foundational research does. It creates the foundation for plausibility—nothing more, nothing less. And it helps you get the story started.

"But, Michael, there's so much to research! Are you saying that writers shouldn't research at all?"

Not at all. Let's get to the efficiency argument.

METHOD #2: JUST-IN-TIME RESEARCH

Once you've made it through the gate, your writing journey begins. There will be many times throughout writing the book that you'll need to stop and do research.

That's where just-in-time research comes in. You research topics as they come up.

It takes some getting used to, but this method is way more efficient.

It's easy to spend weeks researching something, only not to need it in your book. Writers amass notebooks full of interesting factoids that never leave the notebooks. They do one of two things when this happens: they either feel defeated because they wasted time, or they try to find ways to cram all their research into the novel ("I spent all this time reading those history books, damn it, and I'm not going to waste it!")

Just-in-time research eliminates this risk entirely, ensuring that you only research the items that will actually end up in your book.

Most of your research should be just-in-time research. This will help keep you producing words every day, with interruptions here and there as needed.

Just-in-time research is like a speed bump. It slows you

down, but just for a few seconds. Go too fast over it, though, and you'll mess up your shocks.

To give another example from my *Android X* series, there's a chapter in the book where one of the protagonists visits an attorney's office. I've been to many law offices in my life, but I had to think hard about what one would look like in the year 2300. So I had to take a few minutes to do some Google research on what law offices look like today, and then do some brainstorming on what would change. First, there wouldn't be any books or bookshelves, which are an iconic symbol of law offices today. After a bit of brainstorming, I decided that law offices probably wouldn't even exist. Artificial intelligence would eliminate the need for receptionists, paralegals, and lawyers, replacing them with algorithms that instead would advocate for clients based on factual details. I came up with the idea that people in the future would visit "virtual" law offices in the year 2300, and instead of interacting with real attorneys, they would interact with "robo attorneys" who looked human but were really just avatars of a hyper-advanced algorithm. The few human attorneys that did exist would handle only unique cases and function more like engineers of their firms' algorithms.

About 30 minutes later, I was writing again. That's a good example of just-in-time research.

I'll bet that if I added up all the time I spent doing just-in-time research throughout a novel, it would equal several hours, maybe more. It's still research, but it's directed and intentional. That's how you improve your efficiency and the quality of your writing at the same time.

THE POWER OF ANCHOR CONTENT

If you wanted, you could read the works of every expert in the subject matter areas of your book. Some writers do that, but you and I can agree that that's too time-consuming. Right? Right?

Instead, consider what I call "anchor content." Anchor content is content that by itself forms the foundation of your foundational research. It should be the first place you consult whenever you do just-in-time research. For my *Android X* series, my anchor content was the two books I mentioned by Michio Kaku and Cecily Sommers.

Think of anchor content like a mentor. It's there whenever you need advice.

Whenever I had a situation of just-in-time research, I consulted those books first to see if they commented on what I needed. Most of the time, there was something there that I could use as a starting point for a brainstorming session without having to do additional research. If the books were silent, I looked outside of them for guidance. In other words, the anchor content "anchored" me from doing extraneous research.

Another benefit of anchor content is that if you pick the right content, it helps you create a unified theme in your story. For example, I'm a big fan of Michio Kaku, and I like to think that he and I share the same outlook for the future. As a result, my series is quite positive in how it treats android technology and artificial intelligence. A lot of Kaku's concepts informed the way I think about the future, and so you'll find them pop up now and again in my book—mixed in with my own philosophies, of course.

This is why I'm an advocate of finding popular nonfiction books as a starting point for your research wherever possible. They help you think bigger and broader and eliminate a lot of manual work on your part.

Popular nonfiction books are extremely focused on one or two concepts, targeted at a general audience. Authors like Bill

Bryson, Daniel Pink, Malcolm Gladwell write popular nonfiction.

I once read a book called *Sand* by Michael Welland. The book is about the history and science of sand. Seriously.

Popular nonfiction is often written in an easy-to-understand style, and the authors break concepts down so that everyday people can understand them and use them to improve their lives. Another benefit of popular nonfiction is that it's usually available in e-book and audiobook format, which helps you consume it faster.

Yet another benefit of popular nonfiction is that despite its simple approach, it is thoroughly researched, so much of the difficult stuff has already been done for you. All you have to do is find the right book. Most of them also include references and sources, so if there was ever a concept you wanted to explore further, you could use those as jumping-off points.

In other words, popular nonfiction makes great anchor content and can save you time and effort, thus allowing you to focus on writing.

Remember too that every novel is different and requires different research demands. Maybe the anchor content you need isn't a book. Maybe it's a series of TED Talks, or YouTube videos, or a documentary. Do what works for you.

HOW DETAILED SHOULD YOUR NOTES BE?

If you take notes, they should be detailed enough to help you remember what you researched so that you can incorporate them into your book later.

Here are some other things to consider when taking your notes:

- Always be asking "what if" when you're

researching. It's the sole question that will help you find the info you need and also fuel your creativity.

- See a scene, person, place, or thing that you want to put in your story? When you encounter it, capture it in the five senses. What does it look, smell, feel, taste, and sound like? Capturing it in five dimensions now will make it super easy to import it into your story later, especially when you're in the murky middle of your novel and your brain isn't working.

MY STEP-BY-STEP GUIDE TO RESEARCH

Here's a series of steps to ensure that you don't get bogged down by research.

Foundational Research

1. Map out one or two subject areas that you need to understand to start writing. Spend no more than 30 minutes on this.
2. Figure out who the pre-eminent experts are for each of those subject areas. Pick one expert per subject area.
3. Buy/borrow one key book from those experts and find your anchor content. If those experts happen to have podcast interviews, blog articles, YouTube videos, or TED Talks, allow yourself up to two hours consuming their content in addition to reading their books. If you don't like the content, find another expert.
4. Determine how long it will take you to get through the material. Every novel is different, but remember:

writers write. Beware of spending all your time researching. Set a hard deadline.

5. Consume the content quickly, taking detailed but not extensive notes. Organize the notes logically so that you can easily reference them later. (But don't procrastinate when organizing. Do it quickly.)
6. Meet (or beat) your deadline. Then, start writing.

Just-in-Time Research

1. Write your novel.
2. Whenever you come across something you're not sure about in your story, consult your anchor content first. If you cannot find what you need in your anchor content, branch out and do more research, but set a timer and don't allow yourself to spend too much time researching. Find what you need, make sure that you understand it, take quick notes, and get back to writing as soon as possible.
3. Implement the research into your writing.
4. Rinse and repeat.

Remember, it's better to take the time to research issues that come up in your manuscript *immediately when they arise.* Resist the urge to go sloppy. You'll thank me when you finish your novel in record time.

It's much easier to fix a problem while it's fresh in your mind than waiting to address it later.

I know that it seems counterintuitive to do research this way, but you'll be amazed how much time you'll save. It will also be amazing how well your research will help you captivate your readers.

WRITING YOUR NOVEL: HOW TO WRITE, WHAT TO WRITE, AND WHEN

WHAT TO PREPARE BEFORE YOU START YOUR NOVEL

Are you ready to write? Of course you are!

I'll hold your hand through the entire process, and I'll teach you what to expect. Don't be afraid to use this book as a reference while you are writing your manuscript. You may need it.

Here's what you need to finalize before you start writing.

First, it helps to know the opening scene. How does the novel start? Though not required, you'll do better if you have a sense of how you will start.

Second, finish your foundational research.

Third, you'll need your outline...that you'll create *while* you write. More on that soon—just remember that I said it.

After that, you're ready to start.

Don't make starting your book ceremonious. Don't announce to all your social media networks with great fanfare that you're starting your book. Don't make checklists of everything you need to do. These are subconscious forms of procrastination.

Just take a deep breath, sit down at your computer, and start writing. That's what professional writers do. They're very unemotional about it. To them, starting a new book is as mundane as starting a load of laundry. It's just something they *do*, and no one gives them a pat on the back. Readers might give them wads of money when they publish that book, though!

That's all you need to get started. Recognize your emotions because you're probably excited, nervous, scared, and uncertain about how this is going to go. Any emotions you may be feeling are normal.

Relax as much as you can and enjoy the moment. Be prepared to listen to your creative voice, have fun, go with the flow, and venture wherever your story takes you with whatever techniques your creative voice tells you to use.

Are you ready?

Here we go...

EDITING AS YOU GO: THE ULTIMATE GUIDE TO LOOPING/CYCLING

There's a concept in *Writing into the Dark* called cycling. I call it looping.

Here's how it works: when you write 500 words, you stop, go back through what you wrote, making corrections here and there until you reach the point where you left off.

You do this every 500 words, and it's the best tool for writing in one draft because you're constantly going back over your story.

Looping has many benefits:

- You strengthen the story as you go.
- You catch typos and grammatical errors.
- You catch inconsistent character details, like accidentally switching eye colors.
- You catch plot inconsistencies, like realizing you need to set something up. This will require you to loop further back.
- You catch issues like passive voice, showing versus telling, and other common problems that you miss while you're writing it the first time.

Looping is the engine that gives writing into the dark force. Without it, you would have no choice but to rewrite. Yet, when most people hear "writing in one draft," they don't think about looping. Writing into the dark gets a bad rap because of it.

With looping, you don't actually write your book on one draft. It just *feels* like it. You're actually writing multiple drafts; you're just doing it strategically.

I loop through my chapters multiple times before the end.

There are three types of looping:

- Looping while you're writing. This is what you'll be doing most of the time.
- Looping to fix a character or plot detail. You will do this a lot.
- Looping to finalize the story. I call this a master loop —more on that later.

Writers often have many questions about looping. How do you do it? What do you look for? How do you know what to fix?

Most writers I know just reread what they wrote and fix anything that seems out of place. They might rewrite a couple of sentences, add additional description or sensory details, remove details that don't make sense, fix typos, and many other things. They just go with the flow.

That's what you should do too. Don't make it harder than it should be. Looping is not something that should be too time or energy-intensive. Just review what you wrote, make minor changes, and move on. If you can't do that, then find ways to minimize your critical voice because it likely has too much power over you.

If you're spending hours in one loop, then you're doing it wrong.

Let's go through some looping scenarios so that you know how to handle them.

LOOPING SCENARIO #1: THE STANDARD LOOP

You start writing. After 552 words, you arrive at a turn of thought or a good stopping point. Your creative voice will gently stop you.

It's time to loop. Go back through the 552 words and simply read them and look for corrections.

Then, proceed to the end and start writing again.

This is how your looping will go around 80 percent of the time.

Oh, and you'll notice I said 552 words, not 500. 500 is not a hard or fast rule. Sometimes you'll be in flow and write well past the 500. Or, you may finish a section shortly before you hit 500. Both are fine. Just listen to your creative voice's pause. It'll tell you when to start looping.

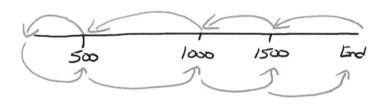

View in high resolution at
www.authorlevelup.com/pantsingimages

If you're still struggling with *how* to do this, and the "just read it and make corrections" advice doesn't work with your personality type, try this.

Consider looping items in isolation. There are certain items you can check for when you loop if you need some more structure:

- loop for plot
- loop for character details
- loop to improve sensory details/descriptions
- loop for dialogue

Essentially, you're doing loops within a loop. You can go overboard here. But sometimes I find that I will review a section a couple of different times, looking for plot the first time, character details the next, and so on. I loop the chapter several times in one go.

This may help you if you struggle to review everything at once. Over time, you may find that you no longer need to loop items in isolation.

LOOPING SCENARIO #2: PLOT FIX

You'll be writing, and suddenly, you'll realize you screwed something up with the plot. Maybe your creative voice takes you down a path you didn't expect and requires you to fix a minor detail earlier in the book.

For example, I wrote a novel where the hero agrees to meet a love interest for ice cream. He tells her to meet him at a local park next to the shop. What did I have him do? Instead, he just met her at the shop. Oops! I had to go back and fix that. Easy fix, but an important detail.

When you fix details, it's a good idea to read a few hundred words before and after to catch any other residual errors that might be left over. This is also a perfect opportunity to review the section again.

Don't go overboard, though. The pace of a loop

should be brisk—stay long enough to fix the problem correctly, take a look at everything else to make sure your fix doesn't break anything else in the story, and then move on.

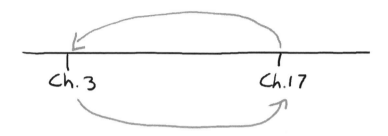

View in high resolution at
www.authorlevelup.com/pantsingimages

LOOPING SCENARIO #3: CHARACTER FIX

This scenario is similar to the previous one, but it usually involves discovering that you have an inconsistent character detail that needs to be fixed throughout the novel. For example, your hero's eyes might be brown in chapter one and black in chapter sixteen, or a character has changed clothes, but you forgot to mention it. These types of errors will pull a reader out of the story.

The key is to fix the problem everywhere. This means checking the last instance you described your character and looking at every other place you describe them. This takes time, and it will likely take you through several sections of the novel. Take your time, loop the sections you fix, update your reverse outline (we'll discuss in the next chapter), and get back to writing as soon as you can.

Remember to fix character problems as soon as they come up while they're fresh in your mind!

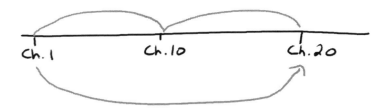

View in high resolution at
www.authorlevelup.com/pantsingimages

IT'S OKAY TO JUMP AROUND A LOT

Many writers who write this way for the first time second-guess whether they're doing it correctly. They find themselves jumping around *a lot* and fixing lots of details. This leads them to think they're doing it wrong.

Jumping around a lot is okay, and it's how this method works. I'd be more concerned if you *weren't* jumping around a lot.

Writing this way can be messy. Accept that and trust the process.

A FEW WORDS ON LOOPING FREQUENCY

I find that I loop more often in the first quarter and the least often in the last quarter.

In the first quarter, I loop every 500 words or so, as recommended in *Writing into the Dark.*

In the last quarter, I loop every 1,000 words or so. This helps me get to the end faster.

There's no right or wrong way. Flex your looping based on

how the novel is going—just make sure you don't stop. Otherwise, you'll have more work to do to prepare the book for your editor, and that's exactly what we want to avoid!

FINAL WORDS ON LOOPING

Let these be your guiding stars when you loop:

- Be diligent with looping throughout the entire novel. It's okay to skip a looping session or two if your creative voice is humming along, but make sure you keep doing it regularly.
- Loop briskly. Don't fall into the trap of rewriting. You're just looking for typos, inconsistent details. If you find a plot hole that does require substantial changes, make them, but make them quickly.

"DOCUMENTING" YOUR STORY: WHY YOU SHOULD OUTLINE YOUR NOVEL AS YOU GO

Writing into the Dark covers "reverse outlines," which are outlines that you create as you go. This is another critical part of the writing into the dark method.

Remember our goals:

- to write well
- to write cleanly
- to write efficiently

The reverse outline helps us write well and efficiently.

Think about it: is it efficient to spend a bunch of time creating an outline, only not to follow some or all of it when you start writing? In the traditional outlining method (which happens before writing), you expend a lot of energy that may not end up in the manuscript. Maybe it helps you learn your world or characters more, maybe not.

With a reverse outline, *everything* you write will end up in the outline. There's no waste. Reverse outlines are always 100 percent accurate.

Why do a reverse outline? Here is why I use them:

- They help me "document" the story as I go.
- If I ever need to remember what happened in a story, I can just refer to the outline.
- They help me manage character and setting details.
- They help me manage my series.

Reverse outlining is a critical skill you must develop if you want to use this method. It will help you keep everything straight.

This is one of the great techniques behind writing a novel in one draft too.

COMMON QUESTIONS ABOUT REVERSE OUTLINING

Q: How do I create a reverse outline?

A: However you want, but I recommend making your reverse outline digital. For basic outlines, I use Scrivener, so I keep my reverse outline as a separate document in my binder. I use the split-screen feature to have my story on the top and the outline on the bottom. For more advanced reverse outlines, I use Microsoft Excel (more on that soon).

I don't recommend pen and paper because even if you digitize your notes, they'll be harder to reference later. If you must do this, use an Optical Character Recognition (OCR) tool to convert your handwriting to text so you can at least search your notes. And even then, it won't be perfect.

Q: Can I use outlining software for my reverse outline (like Plottr or Campfire)?

A: I suppose you could use dedicated outlining software too, but I don't have enough experience with them to comment on them definitively. But sure, read this chapter and see if you can apply it to tools you already have and are familiar with. What matters is that you can create and refer to your outline quickly and easily.

Q: What do I put on the outline?

A: Keep it simple. Here is what I track in my basic outlines:

- chapter number
- POV
- setting
- characters present
- character details introduced
- pacing (optional)
- brief description (2-3 sentences max)

Don't track too much or this will become a chore.

Q: When will I ever need my outline again?

A: You'll need it more often than you think, especially if you write a series. When you start writing sequels, it's helpful to refer to the outline.

Q: How detailed do I need to be?

A: Detailed enough to help you remember the story. My test is, "In three years when I've completely forgotten this story, will the outline help me remember what happened?" It doesn't mean you have to document every little thing—the reverse outline is about helping you see the big picture and the medium picture, so to speak.

Q: How long should outlining a chapter take?

A: A couple of minutes, no more. It usually takes me about two minutes to document a chapter if I do a basic outline, and around five minutes if I'm doing an advanced outline.

Now, let's discuss different outline types and how to create them.

HOW TO CREATE A BASIC REVERSE OUTLINE

Basic reverse outlines are simple.

The easiest way to create a basic reverse outline is to create a separate document and record your story details there.

If your writing app has a binder, simply create a separate document you can use as a reference so it's just a click away.

Your basic outline should live in the same place as your story.

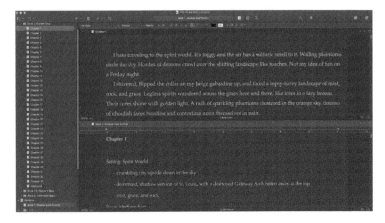

Example of a basic reverse outline in Scrivener using the splitscreen feature. The story is in the top pane and the outline is in the bottom pane. View in high resolution at www. authorlevelup.com/pantsingimages

Here's what I track in my basic outlines, with a description of each element.

Chapter number. Pretty self-explanatory.

Point of view. If the novel has multiple perspectives, it's worth tracking. If you're writing in the first-person with only one viewpoint character, then it's not needed.

Setting. I track where the story takes place. This way, I can do a simple search for all the scenes that take place in a certain setting if needed. I also capture particular details I use so I can remember them later.

Characters present. I write down all the characters in the chapter. This is helpful to see at a glance who is present. I only track major and supporting characters.

Brief description. I aim for concise, 2-3 sentences, though sometimes I go longer than that. The goal is to help me remember what happens in the chapter.

Character details. Whenever I introduce a character, I

capture what they're wearing and any other physical details I need to remember. I also use this section to keep track of any changes in wardrobe, changes to the character's body, and so on.

After I finish a chapter, I fill out the reverse outline.

When do you use basic reverse outlines? I find that they're best suited for:

- short novels (less than 50k)
- short series that you will probably not return to when finished (three books or less)
- stand-alone novels

Here are my rules of thumb when creating a basic reverse outline:

- It doesn't have to be perfect.
- Grammar errors and typos are okay. The focus should be on the story.
- Be detailed but not extensive.

If you'd like to see an example, below are the first four chapters of my novel, *Shadow Deal* (*The Good Necromancer Book 1*). The outline is lightly edited for readability, and I give a little more context to help you understand the story. The actual summaries are a little shorter.

Chapter 1

Setting: Spirit World

- crumbling city upside-down in the sky
- the sky is covered with blistering, wailing phantoms

- a demented, shadow version of St. Louis, Missouri, with a destroyed Gateway Arch bitten away at the top
- mist, grass, and rock

Characters Present: Lester, Cecilia (CeCe), Visgaroth

Summary: Lester, an ex-necromancer down on his luck, arrives in the spirit world for the first time in seven years, and is immediately attacked by Visgaroth, the demon who killed his family seven years ago. He summons his old friend CeCe, who is a lich (a warden of the dead). He and CeCe make their way toward a park, where CeCe uncovers a lake of fresh souls for Lester to review so that he can create an undead servant.

Character Details:

Lester:

- wearing beige gabardine
- bruises on palms, cuts on cheek, knees in pain

CeCe:

- platinum blonde hair
- beautiful human face mixed with skeletal and cadaverous
- red dress with marble spikes jutting out, glittering with diamonds

Visgaroth:

- enormous scorpion with human hands for legs carrying swords

Chapter 2

Setting: Spirit World, CeCe's lake of souls

Characters Present: Lester, CeCe, Bo (unnamed), Visgaroth

Summary: Lester fishes through the lake for a good soul. As soon as he finds a suitable one, Visgaroth attacks, knocking him away from the lake. CeCe attacks Visgaroth, distracting the demon while Lester runs back to the lake. Just before he reestablishes his link with the soul, Visgaroth pins him to the dock. Visgaroth prepares to kill Lester.

Character Details:

- Lester: cuts on his palm, palm is bleeding
- CeCe: using a rose-gold sword
- Visgaroth: Brown scorpion with two main green eyes, both asymmetrical and one bigger than the other, and five pairs of eyes down a football-curved body. Two sets of teeth, one human, one shark-like. Two pincers. Demon head inside its mouth with horns and fiery eyes.

Chapter 3

Setting: Lumière Place Casino, St. Louis

Characters Present: Lester, Rowena, mystery men

Summary: Narrative jumps to before Lester entered the spirit world and the reader learns why he was there. Lester is at the casino for his birthday, drowning his sorrows in cards and alcohol. He is up in a game of blackjack and counting his chips when Rowena slides into the chair next to him, saying she needs help. Lester recognizes her as his dead son's ex-girlfriend, one who he liked very much. Rowena is being chased by mysterious men, and she asks for help. She and Lester escape to the parking garage, where she reveals that she is practicing the dark art of necromancy and the men are trying to stop her. Lester panics because he has left the dark arts for a peaceful life. Mystery men appear literally out of nowhere and knock them down to the floor.

Character Details:

- Lester: Gabardine and driver's cap
- Rowena: Black hoodie, long black hair, olive skin, eyes the color of maple wood

Chapter 4

Setting: Casino Skywalk

Characters Present: Lester, Rowena, Adnan (unnamed)

Summary: Adnan and his gang subdue Rowena. Adnan gives Lester the choice to leave with no consequences, but Lester refuses. The room fills with smoke and Lester faints.

Character Details:

Adnan (unnamed): Black suit, brown hair, mustache and beard, pomaded quiff

Part 2

Setting: Trunk of a car, St. Louis Riverfront

Characters Present: Lester, Rowena, Adnan, mystery shadow

Summary: Lester wakes up in the trunk of a car, listening as Adnan interrogates Rowena, asking her about the location of the corpse she raised. Lester breaks out of the trunk just as Rowena summons the corpse. It wreaks havoc on Adnan and his men, and Adnan throws Rowena into the river. Lester dives in after her, hits his head on a riverbank, and loses sight of Rowena.

Character Details:

Shadow: looks like a grim reaper from behind. Black hoodie.

Part 3

Setting: St. Louis Riverfront, under the Gateway Arch

Characters Present: Lester, two jinn

Summary: Lester wakes up in a bed of gravel, flees from two jinn who have revealed their true forms. Lester has no choice but to enter the spirit world to escape.

Character Details:

Jinn: hair burns like a volcano, eyes like coals, rest of bodies are silhouettes

━━━

You'll notice that I broke Chapter 4 into sections whenever I used section breaks. You don't have to do this; I like it with basic outlines because it helps me be more detailed and doesn't take that much time.

That's how you do a basic outline. Do it as you go, after you finish each chapter. Don't delay. It'll be more accurate and effective if you fill it out while a chapter is fresh in your head.

HOW TO CREATE AN ADVANCED REVERSE OUTLINE

Sometimes, a basic outline isn't enough. Sometimes you need to capture more detail.

The basic reverse outline is what I call a "dead" document. The moment you're done with the novel, it dies. You usually won't need it.

The advanced reverse outline, however, is a living document. You will use it more often.

Let me tell you a story.

I wrote Book 1 of a series and I used a basic outline. The outline captured all the elements I discussed in the previous chapter, and it worked just fine. The story was much more complex than my other series.

I started writing Book 2 but had to stop in the middle of it. I returned three months later to my basic reverse outline. It helped me remember the story, but I forgot the little details. The outline didn't help me because it wasn't detailed enough!

My basic reverse outline completely failed me. I ended up having to do the outline all over again, in a way that would help me charge forward with the story. That's when I created an advanced reverse outline.

You may need an advanced reverse outline when:

- you have a novel that is more complex narratively (multiple POVs, more than two or three subplots, and so on)
- you have a longer series (more than five books)
- you want the ability to see both the macro and micro levels of your story

What do you track with an advanced reverse outline? The same things as with your basic reverse outline. The first difference is that you will capture two summaries—a brief summary and a detailed summary. The second difference is that you will create the outline in Microsoft Excel.

Excel is usually anathema to writers. The thought of using it for *anything* is terrifying for most. However, Excel is an extremely helpful tool for organizing your story quickly and effectively.

For our purposes, it's a few extra steps to use since the outline will live in Excel, but once you're done reading this chapter, I hope you will see why it is worth the effort.

I've created an Advanced Outline template for you. You can download it and follow along by visiting www.authorlevelup.com/advancedoutline. (No email required, just download and enjoy).

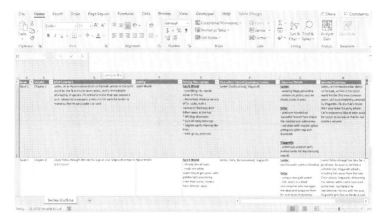

View in high resolution at
www.authorlevelup.com/pantsingimages

I like to use Excel because of sorting and filtering. Let's go through the fields on my sample advanced outline so I can show you how to use it.

Book. The advanced reverse outline gives you the benefit of keeping *all* books in your series in one document. This would be unwieldy in a basic outline. If you want to filter by a particular book, just click the filter button.

Chapter. Also filterable. Want to look at your Chapter 1s for all books in the series. Easy.

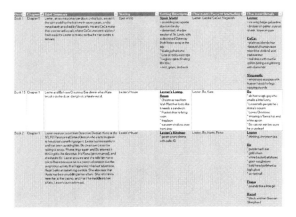

Advanced reverse outline example with the first
three books in a series. The outline is filtered to
Chapter 1 for each book. View in high resolution
at www.authorlevelup.com/pantsingimages

POV. Very, very useful when you have multiple POVs.
Want to see all the chapters from the perspective of a particular
character? Just takes a few clicks.

Brief Summary. Same as the basic outline. I prefer to
keep this column as far to the left as I can. It makes for easier
scanning later.

Setting. I track my settings. The key is to use the same
phrase, in the same way, each time on the spreadsheet. For
example, if a scene takes place in a casino, write "Casino" every
time. Otherwise, your filtering won't work as well.

Setting Details. This is where things start to differ from
the basic outline. I will copy and paste what I wrote about the
setting into the spreadsheet.

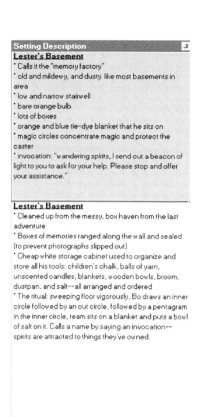

Setting Description

Lester's Basement
* Calls it the "memory factory"
* old and mildewy, and dusty like most basements in area
* low and narrow stairwell
* bare orange bulb
* lots of boxes
* orange and blue tie-dye blanket that he sits on
* magic circles concentrate magic and protect the caster
* invocation: "wandering spirits, I send out a beacon of light to you to ask for your help. Please stop and offer your assistance."

Lester's Basement
* Cleaned up from the messy, box haven from the last adventure
* Boxes of memories ranged along the wall and sealed (to prevent photographs slipped out)
* Cheap white storage cabinet used to organize and store all his tools: children's chalk, balls of yarn, unscented candles, blankets, wooden bowls, broom, dustpan, and salt--all arranged and ordered
* The ritual: sweeping floor vigorously, Bo draws an inner circle followed by an out circle, followed by a pentagram in the inner circle, team sits on a blanket and puts a bowl of salt on it. Calls a name by saying an invocation-- spirits are attracted to things they've owned.

Example of two different chapters that take place in the same setting on an advanced reverse outline. The spreadsheet is filtered by "Lester's Basement." View in high resolution at www. authorlevelup.com/pantsingimages

Proficient Excel users will immediately call me out on how I'm doing this, because it is quite inelegant. I know that. But it still filters well if you search by setting name.

Characters Present. Self-explanatory. If I wanted to execute this field properly, I would have created columns for each character and then simply marked it with an "x." I chose not to do this so I could save time. It still filters well this way.

Character Details. I do the same thing here as I do in the Setting Details field. The key to doing this correctly is to only use the character name to signify them. This way, they will filter properly. Otherwise, your filters will pick up any time the character name is mentioned.

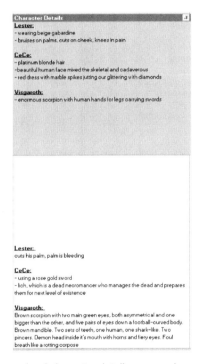

Example of character details on an advanced reverse outline. View in high resolution at www. authorlevelup.com/pantsingimages

And finally, we have a Detailed Summary. In this field, I write detailed paragraphs of what happens in the chapter (also known as "beats.") I capture as much detail as possible without going overboard. This helps me when I need more information about a chapter, but I don't necessarily want to read that chapter. It saves time. I only need to read the chapter if it's not covered in the detailed summary.

Detailed Summary
Lester receives a call from Detective Damian Harris at the STLPD Paranormal Crimes Division who wants to speak to him about something urgent. Lester has reservations and has been avoiding him. Bo chastises Lester for talking to a cop. Phone rings again and Bo answers it thinking it is the detective. It is Fiona (yet unnamed), and she insults Bo. Lester answers and she tells him not to talk to Harris because he is a person of interest due the suspicious activity that happened in his last adventure. Hazel barks at something outside. She also says that Harris has been muddling in her affairs. She tells him to meet her at the casino, or Lester's toast.

Detailed summary example on an advanced reverse outline. View in high resolution at www. authorlevelup.com/pantsingimages

THREE PRACTICAL SCENARIOS ON HOW TO USE THE ADVANCED REVERSE OUTLINE

Let's say you are writing, and you're somewhere around the halfway mark of the novel. Your character arrives at a setting that you introduced earlier in the book, but you can't remember one minor detail you wrote about the setting. For instance, was it day or night, and what color was that building again?

You would filter the outline by the setting details and then review every instance of how you described that particular setting.

Let's say that you uncover an inconsistent character detail that makes you realize you need to know exactly how you described a character throughout the book.

You would filter the spreadsheet in the character detail field, which would give you a snapshot of everything you wrote.

(Also, this is a smart thing to do when you're starting a new book in a series. Review what you wrote for a character or setting *previously* before you introduce it in the new book.)

Let's say you're writing your story. If you can remember to do it, a smart tactic is to reference your outline every time you repeat a character or setting.

For example, if you introduce a supporting character in Chapter 2, and again in Chapter 6, check your outline to remember how you described her *before* you write her into Chapter 6. Then, when she appears in Chapter 7, do it again.

It's extra work, but it's amazing how you forget little details. Trust me on this...

These are the most practical ways the outline will help you. You'll find other ways too.

The advanced reverse outline is something I didn't develop until after 20 novels written into the dark. Now, it is one of my secret weapons. If you use it correctly, I'm sure it will be a secret weapon for you too.

Download your template at www.authorlevelup.com/advancedoutline and feel free to customize it to your liking. Just remember—if you're spending a bunch of time making it pretty or more detailed, you should probably be writing. Don't let this become a path to procrastination!

ADVANCED TIP FOR SERIES

When you write sequels in your series, you have a responsibility to keep your details consistent. Your advanced reverse outline is how you do it, combined with looping.

Here's what I do: when I finish a chapter, I loop back and reread the chapter of the same number in the previous books in my advanced reverse outline.

For example, let's say I'm writing book three in a series, and I finish chapter one.

I will loop that chapter as usual, but then I will go back and (quickly) read chapter one in books one and two as well on my outline. I don't spend much time doing this.

The advanced reverse outline might look like this:

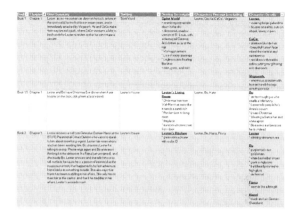

View in high resolution at
www.authorlevelup.com/pantsingimages

I like doing this because it helps me see how all the novels in the series progress. I know which ones progress faster and slower, and it's helpful data in many ways.

The act of reading and writing your story out of sequence is useful because it forces you to make connections you wouldn't otherwise think about.

This tactic takes a little extra time, but it helps you keep everything consistent. Or, you might realize that you need to fix something!

Why do this?

First, you may not write your sequels immediately after one another. You might take breaks between them. The first things your brain will forget are the little details. Unfortunately for us, the little details are the first things readers notice. Also, consider that while you may take time off between novels, your readers are likely to read the books one right after the other if they like your series. That makes little inconsistencies that much more glaring.

Second, it pays to think of your series globally as a single unit. You want everything to be consistent across all books. This exercise will help you do that.

Third, your editor will not save you. They edit many, many books. Unless you send your entire series to them at the same time (which is not practical for most), it's not reasonable for them to keep all the details straight in your sequels. That's your job, and you need all the help you can get.

Like I said, this technique takes a little extra time, but you will be surprised at how interconnected your books are.

0-25%: THE HONEYMOON PHASE AND THE HORRIBLE ROUGH SPOT THAT COMES AFTER

Now that we've covered looping and reverse outlining, it's time to start writing. Let's go through the different areas of the novel and important things to keep in mind as you're drafting. The first and most important area is the 0 to 25 percent mark.

When I was at college, I used to drive from Indianola, Iowa to my hometown of St. Louis, Missouri. The drive was around six hours.

Whenever I got on the road, I always felt pretty good. I had my music picked out. I'd stop at the gas station, fill up my car, and buy some snacks. Then I'd hit the road, excited to be going home.

During the first hour, the drive would be interesting. I'd notice weird houses or cows or presidential campaign signs in the middle of cornfields. The hour would fly by. After the first hour, the reality that I was on a long drive would set in. Every few minutes, I'd gaze at the clock, sighing because only a few minutes had passed. The road signs advertising the next town seemed to spring up every mile.

Iowa City: 87 miles

Iowa City: 86 miles

Iowa City: 85 miles...

And then, the road trip would become dreadful.

Why do I share this?

The first 25 percent of your novel will probably go butter smooth. Everything will hum along, you'll be happy, and you'll be so excited to share the novel with the world. But somewhere around the 25 percent mark, you'll suddenly feel as if you have no idea what you're doing. The uncertainty will hit you hard. You will question everything you ever knew about writing and writing craft. You may even get the urge to quit the novel, possibly your writing career.

Sorry to rain on your nice road trip, but I'd rather you know now so you can be ready for it.

So what do we need to do right now?

We're not at the 25 percent mark yet, so for now, relax and enjoy the words. You're going to be cruising, and it's a wonderful feeling.

Again, this will last until approximately the 25 percent mark, on average. Sometimes, the feeling will last a little less; sometimes, a little longer. But it always ends in the first quarter. Always. My experience is that it often strikes somewhere between 15 and 25 percent.

I cannot understate this enough: the moment after the euphoria wears off is pretty horrible. Almost no one is ever truly prepared for just how hard it will hit them. If you're not strong enough, you'll go crawling back to outlining. You'll never attempt writing into the dark again. At least, that's what I suspect happens to many who attempt this method.

However, while the end of the first quarter is rough and

seemingly hits out of nowhere, there are some subtle warnings before you get there. Use these as rules of thumb:

When you experience your first cloudy sky visibility, start getting ready for the first rough spot. This means that you won't be able to see as far into the novel. You might have a doubt floating around in your head about what a character might do next, a setting, or something else. Wherever that moment is, it's usually where your visibility will shift from cloudy to stormy.

Sometimes, you'll have clear sky visibility beyond the first quarter. You may know what will happen, but you won't feel confident about it. You may doubt a fight scene or a meeting with an important character. So, while your visibility is fine, the words come slower from your fingers.

The first rough spot tends to happen after you've established all the major plot lines and characters. Generally, you introduce (most) major characters before the 25 percent mark. I like to think about this as a confluence; all the characters and plot lines are now converging together and your creative voice has to figure out how to manage them. Put another way, it's like a traffic jam of ideas, and your creative voice is a police officer directing traffic. Eventually, it clears, but every car has to get through first.

You won't know the reason for the first spot. Once you get through the rough spot, you'll wonder why you ever slowed down.

To continue the traffic jam analogy, have you ever been in a traffic jam that was bumper-to-bumper, only for it to suddenly clear up? You look around to see what the cause of the jam was, but you can't find one... The first rough spot is (often) like that. You won't know why you got blocked other than that it was probably your critical voice trying to stop you.

You see, the critical voice doesn't like you making progress. It will throw everything it can at you to make you doubt yourself and retreat into security. Keep that in mind too.

The next question you're probably thinking is, "Okay, I understand. But how do I get through the rough spot?"

Write the next sentence. That's all you can do. It's absolutely true, but absolutely hard if you've never been in this situation before. But it is the best answer.

How do you write the next sentence if you don't know what's next?

You have three choices:

1. Look at what you previously wrote.
2. Take a small break.
3. Sit in the chair and grind.

THE NEAREST ANSWER IS BEHIND YOU

Sometimes, the nearest answer is behind you. It's like when you're on an airplane and the flight attendant says that the nearest exit may be behind you in an emergency. Same concept.

Review the last three chapters you wrote before you encountered your rough spot. More often than not, the answer to where you need to go is somewhere within those pages.

I can't tell you how many times this has been true for me. More times than I can count. It may be true for you too.

This is especially true if you've been away from your novel for an extended period. You'll forget what you wrote, even if your memory is good.

This is another reason why looping is a smart technique. It keeps you in constant contact with what you wrote previously.

TAKE A BREAK

Don't misunderstand me. I'm not saying to quit. Instead, consider taking a "power" break—a break that lasts only a few hours at a time.

One of my favorite strategies is doing a manual activity. If I get stuck in my story, I'll get out my lawnmower and mow the lawn. That's great thinking time for me. Sometimes I mow in silence; other times I listen to music or a podcast. Often, I find that I'll see a fuzzy image of where I need to take the story next.

Taking a nice long shower works too. I read a writer once who said that the best ideas come in the bed, the bathtub, and on the bus. That's true for me!

Taking a long drive is also helpful. So is painting a room, going to the gym, going for a run, gardening, or cleaning your kitchen, or organizing a messy closet. It doesn't matter. Do something manual to get your heart rate going, your lungs pumping, and your mind working.

Sleeping is also a helpful creative aid. If I go to bed with the intention of working out my problem in my sleep, I find that I attract solutions. The act of sleeping rests your brain, which is sometimes all you need to fuel your creative voice.

Another tactic you can use is to expose yourself to new people, places, and activities. Go somewhere you've never gone before with your spouse, significant other, friends, or family. Allow yourself to live in the moment and see if something inspires you.

I have a little game that I play with myself that helps me through rough spots. When I'm in a staring match with the blinking cursor, I pick a piece of media to consume—a book, YouTube video, podcast, or movie. It doesn't matter. Then I tell myself that the answer lies in whatever I consume. Once, when I was stuck in a novel, I surfed YouTube and came across a video about Venus flytraps. It talked about the biology of the plants and how to care for them. It was fascinating. Guess what I wrote into my story when I got back to my computer? Yep, Venus flytraps. Turns out that a Venus flytrap was the key to moving forward in one of my stories. That little game I play helps me through rough spots. And it's fun!

Whatever you do, do NOT walk away from your story for more than a day! It will make it much harder for you to restart. If you take a break, make it short and intentional. Of course, life happens, but keep your consistency going. Otherwise, you'll wake up one day several years later and have made no progress in your story. This tactic requires mental discipline. If you can't do that, don't take a break. You've been warned.

SIT IN THE CHAIR AND GRIND

You may find that looking behind you or taking a break isn't effective, and that's okay too. If that happens, though, it means that you have to sit down and power through it.

Write the next sentence. You do that by following your fingers. Your creative voice *knows* what to write. You just need to learn how to identify its whisper. It'll be hard to hear because the critical voice is screaming at you.

A helpful tactic I've used to "follow my fingers" is to use microfocus. When the other strategies aren't working, and you're losing hope, try this one.

What is the very next thing your character has to do or say? Focus on that. Forget about the overall plot. Forget about feeling tired. Just write that next thing.

Then, what's the *next* thing the character has to do? Write that.

Remember the equation: consistency + curiosity + tenacity = success. It will be your guide here.

Rough spots don't last forever. My experience is that they

only last a few chapters, maybe a few thousand words. Then they dissipate and you're cruising again.

If you practice **consistency** in sitting down regularly and typing even when it's hard, you will eventually emerge on the other end of the rough spot. Like I said, they don't last forever and the math is on your side.

If you practice **curiosity** and learning to hear your creative voice and what it needs, you'll discover the solution.

If you practice **tenacity** and don't give up, you will also emerge on the other side of the rough spot. Many, many writers give up. If you don't, you'll keep going.

All of this is easy to say, but much harder to do.

Once you complete your first rough spot, you'll be much better at navigating them. But boy, that first one will be rough.

Rough spots never go away—you will continue to deal with them in every novel you write. The good thing is that they all have predictable patterns, and the more you write, the more equipped you'll be to deal with them.

These days, rough spots only slow me down for a couple of days, if that. Then I'm back to regular writing speed. I almost always see them coming, and there's very little I haven't encountered. The same will be true for you too. You just have to survive your first one.

REMEMBER THE ROOT CAUSES OF WRITER'S BLOCK AND EMOTIONAL UNDERCURRENTS

Remember the three root causes of writer's block:

- Fear
- Lack of inspiration
- Personal circumstances

Consider whether any of these factors are at play, and if so, use the solutions I talked about in the Mindset chapter.

Also, don't forget about emotional undercurrents. They will factor into your rough spot too. This spot is one of the most dangerous for emotional undercurrents.

It's a perfect storm: you can't see where your story is going, you feel bad about it, and you're not confident about the words you're writing. Very dangerous, and why so many quit.

BRINGING IT ALL TOGETHER

- When you start the novel, you will feel euphoric. Your words will come easily.
- Somewhere around the first quarter, you will suddenly not know what to write next. That's normal, and you will be able to see this moment coming when you have your first cloudy sky visibility day.
- You have three options when you encounter your first rough spot: look behind you to find the answer in previous chapters, take a short break, or sit in the chair and grind.
- If you're suffering from writer's block, remember to look for the appropriate root cause.
- Beware emotional undercurrents. They'll sabotage you if you lose track of them.

You can do it. Just keep going.

25-75%: WHEN THE NOVEL BECOMES REAL

Once you make it past your first rough spot, you'll be somewhere north of the 25 percent mark. Between here and the 75 percent mark, you'll use the same tactics.

First, you'll keep writing.

Second, you'll deal with rough spots as they come up using the tactics I discussed in the prior chapter. There's nothing unusual you'll encounter between the 25 and 75 percent mark that you don't already have the tools to deal with.

The only difference will be that you will probably have cloudier visibility and the rough spots will be a little different. No rough spot is the same. However, my experience is that after the first rough spot, the subsequent ones are smaller. They're usually just logistic problems you have to solve, such as figuring out how to get a character from point A to point B, or discovering what your villain's true motives are.

If you want this section of the novel to go smoothly, do a few things:

- Write consistently. Keep making progress on the

novel every day, even in rough spots. Having a daily minimum word count will help you.

- Don't get sloppy.
- Don't get lazy. Keep focused on writing well– staying deep inside your characters' heads. One of the great dangers here is losing stamina. Readers need sensory details and depth to stay invested in your story.
- Deal with rough spots ruthlessly. Don't let them derail you.
- Keep looping. Stay diligent with it. It'll help you with the rough spots.

Be on the lookout for some other helpful mile markers as you're writing. The one I look for is the midpoint, which is usually the moment where the hero goes from reactive to proactive. Lately, my novels have had rough spots around the midpoint. Yours may too.

The best strategy for this section is to enjoy the journey, deal with the rough spots, and manage your emotions and stamina. Do that and you'll be just fine.

75-100%: THE GLIMMER AND THE MAD DASH AFTERWARD

Another important moment near the end of the story doesn't have anything to do with plot. Instead, it has to do with the ending.

I call it the "glimmer": it's when you suddenly know exactly how the novel is going to end. You see all the plotlines converging and you know what you need to do, where the character needs to go, and what the final scenes will be.

The glimmer is an amazing phenomenon. You've been writing into the dark for an entire novel, and now you're not in the dark. You no longer have to worry about visibility issues, which is a relief!

You will still have a rough spot or two, but they won't be nearly as difficult. Again, they'll often be logistical issues, which are easily solved.

I find that the glimmer usually happens around the 75 percent mark, but I have seen it as early as 60 percent and as late as 90 percent.

When you see it, you have two choices:

- Write like hell and finish the novel.

- Maintain your current writing speed and arrive at the ending steadily.

Both have pros and cons.

If you decide to write like hell, the same rules apply. Remember, you're only writing one draft, so even if you write like hell, you still have a responsibility to write well, cleanly, and efficiently. Otherwise, you'll waste time and effort. Of course, I won't lie—there's something to be said about ramping up your speed so you can finish the novel.

However, there are two things that you *can* stop doing when you see the glimmer: documenting and looping. By giving up on these, you'll be able to write faster. You can write down what happens in your chapters when you're done. At this point, you're close enough to the end that it won't be a tedious task to outline a bunch of chapters at once.

Looping is optional too. You can also cover these chapters with a final master loop that I'll discuss later.

Sometimes, it's wise to keep your current pace when you see the glimmer. If you do, you will have documented all your chapters and looped them properly once you write "The End." That's supremely satisfying.

It's your choice. There's no right or wrong way. But if the spirit moves you to write like crazy, then obey.

I've done it both ways. With most of my novels, I just write quickly to the end. But with more complex novels that have more plotlines and characters to manage, I like to keep my current pace because the story benefits from more looping sessions.

Either way, have fun in this section. Final battles are always fun to write, and I like writing denouements too. Pretty soon, you're going to have a finished novel, so enjoy that. Expect a rough spot or two, but you'll be just fine.

FREQUENTLY ASKED QUESTIONS THAT COME UP DURING THE WRITING PROCESS

Here are some miscellaneous frequently asked questions about pantsing that you may still have.

Q: How much pre-planning should I do before starting the novel?

A: A common question that comes up is *when* to start writing. When do you know you're ready? After all, you're not going to outline, so what does one need to do?

I recommend knowing what the opening scene is going to be. What problem is your hero going to deal with? I often start with a snapshot in my head of that very first scene, maybe the first chapter. I start with that, and move on. You don't need to be able to "see" far into the story. Just that first scene. Then, you trust your creative voice from there.

Q: Should I do character sketches before I start writing?

A: It's up to you, but remember the tenets of pantsing and writing into the dark: you write to discover the story. I don't think character sketches will help you at the micro-level. The micro-level (i.e., the words on the page) are what readers identify with, and you can't plan for that. Instead of doing character sketches, I'd rather spend my time writing, but that's just me.

Q: What if my writing sucks?

A: The question is, "sucks according to whom?" You? Your friends and family? Other writers (who aren't paying readers)? Or true readers?

I have received many emails from writers who are not sure if their writing has what it takes. All of these writers did not publish their books yet when they emailed me.

My question for you is, "If you don't publish the book, how will you ever know how readers will react?" Maybe they *won't* buy it, but that doesn't mean your writing is bad. Or, maybe they'll surprise you.

I'm a big fan of living a life with no regrets. If you don't publish your book, you'll regret it and spend your life wondering what if.

Write the best novel you can, follow the advice in this book to create the best-written story you can, recruit beta readers, hire a good copyeditor and proofreader, and publish the damn book. If it fails, welcome to the luxurious, highly prestigious club of first-time authors whose books didn't meet their expectations. It's a badge of honor.

But you won't know anything until you publish.

The US comedian and radio host Steve Harvey said something in an interview that always stuck with me. He talked about how you just need to jump if you want to follow your dreams. I'll paraphrase the analogy he used.

You're standing on a cliff on a beautiful sunny day overlooking a valley of rocks so colorful they could have been painted. There's a parachute strapped to your back, and the wind is blowing hard against your face.

Parachuting is scary—what if the chute doesn't open or what if you have a heart attack or what if you get tangled on the rocks or...it doesn't matter. The key is to jump. If you don't, then you're going to stand on that cliff all alone, wondering "what if" while a bunch of other people float by on their parachutes, having the time of their lives.

What an analogy. That's why you need to jump too. Publish the book.

Q: Okay, but seriously—what if I publish and readers dislike the book?

A: I empathize. I know what it's like to write a book that doesn't sell. Learn from it and move on. Find out why they didn't like it. Are there nuggets of truth in their feedback, or did you put the book in front of the wrong readers? Was your cover on-point? How about your book description? How did the readers who disliked the book find yours, and is it the type they normally read? You've got to mine for the signals. As I keep saying, sometimes, it has nothing to do with you or your book. Sometimes, it's just beyond your control. Focus on the things within your control: learning how to improve your craft, continuing to sit down and write even if it's painful, and becoming a better marketer and businessperson. The answer is honestly that easy, but also that hard. Few people in this business become bestsellers with a first book.

Q: How will I know how long my book will be?

A: You won't. You can try to guess, but every time you guess, you'll be wrong!

However, you can use some basic guideposts:

- When you hit your first rough spot, you'll probably be between 15 and 25 percent. Do the math on how many words you've written and multiply it by four.
- When your character goes from reactive to proactive halfway through the book, you're around the 50 percent mark. This isn't always true, but I find that it usually is. At this point, multiply your word count by two.
- When you see the glimmer, count on being between around 75 and 85 percent. Multiply your word count by 1.5.

When you do your multiplication, add 5,000 above and below your calculation. That's your range, and the best you can do, honestly.

That *may* get you a somewhat accurate count. Or, you might be hilariously wrong. Track your guesses and see how good you did. If anything, this exercise will take your mind off the anxiety of book length and give you something more productive to focus on.

Don't stress about word counts. Everything will work out in the end.

Q: How long should my book be?

A: As long as your creative voice says it needs to be. End of story.

Q: How many chapters should my book have?

A: As many as your creative voice says there should be. End of story. Don't stress out about it.

Q: How long should my chapters be?

A: As long as the creative voice says they should be.

"But, Michael, what if they're really, really short?" Look at James Patterson. Case closed.

"But, Michael, what if they're really, really long?" Look at virtually any epic fantasy novel. Case closed.

Like I said, don't stress out over this. There are other things in your novel to worry about. Trust your creative voice and trust the process.

Q: But what if I write a Book 1 that's 50,000 words and a Book 2 that's 40,000 words? Won't readers dislike that?

A: Ah, that's what I call the "Biggie Smalls" problem—when you have books in a series that have vastly different lengths.

Will readers care? I don't know. If Book 1 is 50,000 words and Book 2 is 60,000, I don't think readers will mind. Look at *Harry Potter*—every subsequent book got progressively longer and nobody cared one bit.

But if your book lengths trend downward—I don't know. All I can tell you is that I have had this concern too, and somehow —*somehow,* all my novels in a series end up with similar lengths, give or take 5,000 words. My creative voice always seems to produce books that are of a similar length. I find that very interesting. I've worried about the Biggie Smalls problem too, but it hasn't happened to me yet. If and when it does, I'll probably shrug and publish the book anyway. As long as the story itself satisfies readers, then the length shouldn't matter. And if it does, oh well. Don't make the mistake of padding your book just for length—readers will *definitely* hate that, and frankly, that will hurt your sales more than the Biggie Smalls problem. Keep it in perspective.

Q: What if I can't make up my mind about what should happen in the story?

A: You come to a scene and you see two possible scenarios. Both seem equally viable, but you're paralyzed with indecision on what to do. It happens to new authors. My advice is to pick the path that excites or inspires you the most. Often, that's the choice that scares you.

The next question is, "But what happens if I make the wrong choice?"

I don't think there's any such thing as a wrong choice. The story will mold itself around whatever you choose. This happened to me a few times on my first pantsing runs. Ultimately, I made a choice, stuck to it, and didn't look back. It's easier said than done when you've never dealt with uncertainty before, but trust me that your creative voice will know what to do almost every time. That's why I say that writing into the dark is about having faith in yourself.

But sure, sometimes you might veer into a dead end after a choice. You'll most certainly run into a dead end if you listen to your critical voice. As long as you do the best you can to listen to your creative voice's suggestions, you should be fine. And remember, it's okay to throw away words and backtrack if you need to. Many writers don't like to hear this, but it's true. Your creative voice is like the mouse looking for cheese in the labyrinth. Sometimes it has to backtrack, but it always finds the cheese.

Q: How do I stop getting lost in my story?

A: Are you lost or are you about to discover something amazing? I hear this question a lot from people because they fear that the story is meandering too much. Maybe it is, or maybe it isn't. You don't really know until you're done writing. And even then, I believe it's up to paying readers to decide this, not you. My advice is to keep following your creative voice. And, read my previous answers to the questions above about what to do if you're afraid of readers not liking your work.

Q: What if I have too many ideas and I can't commit to one path?

A: Sometimes, people tell me that they have so many interesting ideas that they jump from novel to novel. They can't commit to writing just one story in the dark—their imagination keeps taking them to new projects. I don't know what to say other than to focus and force yourself to commit. If you're the kind of person who needs to work on multiple stories at the same time, do what suits your personality. But you'll never finish a novel if you don't commit to it. It's entirely up to you.

Q: Is it ever appropriate to give up or put a story on hiatus if you're not feeling it?

A: This is a deeper question than it sounds. I need to answer this on a few levels.

On the surface level, let's talk about short-term breaks. Is it ever appropriate to take a break from a story? Sure, I've taken breaks from stories. When the COVID-19 pandemic hit, I didn't return to my then-current novel for eighteen months. When I was able to focus on fiction again, I picked the story back up, reviewed my outline, and simply wrote the next sentence. I finished the book in two weeks. But boy, those first few days weren't fun. That's why it's much easier if you finish your story straight through. Having to restart adds complexity and additional uncertainty to the process. It's better to charge into the dark and deal with all the trouble that comes with it than to put your story down and return to it many months later. Trust me.

Life is going to happen, but don't let your breaks happen because of writer's block. That's why I wrote this book—to help you through those tough times. If you still struggle with putting stories down, your issues are most likely mental, and you should continue to work on them. You'll get there if you keep trying.

On the next level, let's talk about permanent breaks from your story. My answer is no, it's not really appropriate to give up a story unless there is some other force outside of your writing that forces you to do so. Personal circumstances, injuries, and so on—those are perfectly okay.

I've only ever given up on one story into the dark, and it had nothing to do with writer's block. I was writing a story about a Muslim character and I had him using magic—I discovered that magic use in the Islam religion is a gigantic no-no. I couldn't figure out how to reconcile the story, so I shelved it out of respect for my readers, because I do have Muslim fans. Ultimately, that was my fault for not doing adequate research before I started the novel. (Remember the disengaging elements that I talked about in the character chapter!) Aside from this, I am very strict with myself—I start whatever I finish, and you should too. It's not only a work ethic thing, it's also a personal pride thing. I believe that if a story is worth starting, then it's also worth finishing. I don't like to leave my creative voice hanging.

On an even deeper level, is it ever appropriate to quit writing? Of course not, unless it has to do with life. You've chosen this profession for a reason—every day you don't write is a day you'll wish you did. As I recommended in previous chapters, your issue is most likely mindset, and while I can *tell* you a million times how to beat writer's block and fear, only *you* can do it. How bad do you want to finish your story? How miserable will you be if you don't finish that idea in your head? If you really want to do it, you'll find a way. It's that simple, and also that hard.

Q: How do I develop faith in myself and my work?

A: New converts to pantsing have asked me this over the years. "Michael, I understand that I need to have faith in my work, but how can I do that?"

You just have to take the leap. If you're the type who worries about process, you're never going to be prepared. It's like parenting—you can prepare all you want, but you're never truly prepared to become a parent. The only way you learn parenting is by doing. Pantsing is the same way.

Starting the process in and of itself is an act of faith. Instead of worrying about the process, try to focus on how you'll feel when you finish. Identify the emotions you'll feel, and remember those. They'll keep you going, as well as writing that next sentence.

All you need to supercharge your faith in story is to finish a novel into the dark for the first time. I guarantee you that if you make it past the first time, you'll see the entire process with unbelievable clarity. You will still struggle with areas, but simply finishing one novel without an outline (in one draft, at that) will boost your confidence more than anything else I know.

Q: How can I become a better storyteller?

A: Many writing craft books focus on structure. They teach you the "macro" level of storytelling, but not the "micro" level. In other words, how do you put the black marks on the page in such a way that it captivates readers at the micro level?

The answer is simple, but it does require a lot of work.

First, read like a demon. Read the works of mega-bestsellers and try to deconstruct how they pull off their storytelling magic at the micro level. You can learn more from the pages of a mega-bestseller than 100 writing books combined. Your goal is to become aware of different techniques. Studying the mega-bestsellers can teach you how to move from accidentally writing good scenes to intentionally writing good scenes because you're aware of what you're doing. That doesn't happen overnight.

Second, check out my Writing Craft Playbook. It's a free book I offer that helps you sharpen your eye to spot techniques at the micro level.

Third, take courses from long-term professional writers. Dean Wesley Smith (WMG Publishing), Cat Rambo, Dave Farland, and so on. Learn from the people walking the path you want to walk in the future.

Fourth, write a lot. The more you write, the better you'll get. Every word equals experience. This is also why I dislike rewriting so much. Revising isn't writing!

Fifth, consider finding a mentor who is further down the road. Not someone who will critique your craft and ask you to rewrite stuff, but someone who can offer you craft tips from time to time. The great thing about our community is that there are plenty of successful authors who want to share their wisdom and experience.

Becoming a good storyteller isn't easy. It doesn't happen immediately, but if you're intentional about it, you'll see results over time.

Q: Is it truly possible to become a better storyteller without the help of a developmental editor?

A: A developmental editor is one person with one opinion. How do you know that their opinions are correct? You don't, not any more than you know whether your own decisions are correct.

Developmental editors are going to recommend rewriting and restructuring, and you know how I feel about that.

Plus, how do you prove that a developmental edit *improves* reader enjoyment of a story? I don't believe you can.

Developmental editors are the most expensive editors you

can buy. Are you willing to spend thousands of dollars for one person's opinion (who might not even be right?) *One person* who may or may not have a quantifiable track record in helping authors sell more books?

I receive lots of angry emails from editors (usually developmental editors) about my opinions on this, but I just shrug. This type of editing just isn't compatible with pantsing, not if you want to follow it as outlined in this book. If what I just wrote got under your skin, then this method probably isn't for you.

If you want to spend exorbitant sums of money on someone else's *guesses* about your story, go ahead, but there's no guarantee your book will sell any better than if you don't hire one. A developmental editor could *hurt* your book too. What if following their suggestions made readers put your story down? I never hear anyone ask that question.

I've never met a reader who has said, "I only read books that are developmentally edited" or "I only like books that have a smooth character arc that follows the Hero's Journey." It doesn't happen.

Are there good developmental editors out there? I'm sure there are, but it's probably a small number.

As I said in the previous question, exercise some faith in yourself as a writer and in your work. If you're going to gauge your storytelling skills, do it with paying readers. They'll teach you more than a developmental editor ever can in my opinion. If anything, beta readers are a better option because they're closer to your target audience.

If your story has a structural issue, let readers point it out, learn from it, and apply your knowledge forward to the next story. It's a lot cheaper too.

Q: Is it possible to pants a novel with another writer?

A: Okay, I planted this question because I want to put an idea into the universe to see what happens.

Is it possible to connect two writers' creative voices? I believe it is.

I used to love the show "Whose Line Is It Anyway?" where comedians improvise against each other. They have to sing songs and make up pretend dialogue at a moment's notice. If you watch their skits, it's masterful how two people who have no idea what the skit is going to be can come up with something hilarious and TV-ready—while the cameras are rolling.

Can writers do that? Sure. Here's what I think it could look like.

First, no outlining. Only a couple of introductory sessions between the writers to agree on who the main character, supporting characters, villain, and conflict are. Also, both writers would need to have a loose idea of the world, but not too much. Both writers would need to agree on how the opening scene would start.

Next, Writer A would write the first 1,000 words (using their creative voice) and loop them. It would have to be 1,000 or more words to avoid tedious passing back-and-forth. Then, Writer A passes the manuscript to Writer B, who would read the words and then write the next 1,000 words. Writer B would trust their creative voice, and as a strict rule, would *not* change anything that Writer A wrote unless it was inconsistent or didn't jibe with what comes next.

Writer A would then loop Writer B's words, make corrections, challenge anything that doesn't look right, and then loop back over the entire manuscript. Whoever ends a chapter would have to fill out the reverse outline.

The novel would continue like this until finished. Each section would get looped twice. Both writers might have to hop on a call several times throughout the drafting to settle any issues that come up, especially in rough spots.

Could both writers sync their creative voices? And more importantly, would the book sell? Man, that's a fascinating concept.

Right now, the common wisdom is that collaborated novels should be outlined so that both writers are on the same page. That's probably a good idea. I collaborated with an author friend on a series, and that's how we wrote the story, even though I was writing another series into the dark at the same time. Outlining worked out very well for us.

(That series is called Modern Necromancy if you're interested.)

But two writers who trust each other, the process, and their creative voices could create something cool. The writers would have to be on similar levels, both in emotions and craft. This would fail if one writer completely trusted their creative voice but the other writer didn't, for example.

If you ever try that, email me and let me know how it goes!

PANTSING...ON YOUR PHONE???

Let's talk about an alternative (and maybe advanced) technique for pantsing to help you while writing your novel.

Did you know that you can write novels on your phone? Did you also know that you can write them without an outline?

I write a lot on my phone. With my busy lifestyle, it's the only way I can get words in some days. Before the COVID-19 pandemic, I estimated that approximately 40 percent of all my words came from my phone!

I use the Scrivener and Ulysses iOS apps to write anywhere I go.

The day before I wrote this chapter, I was waiting for a friend at a coffee shop, but she was running late. I pulled out my phone and wrote a few paragraphs while waiting for her. It was around 200 words. My total for the day was around 2,600 words, so my phone contributed to 7 percent of my words for the day!

Writing on your phone is about little bursts here and there. It's 200 words here, 50 words there. Over time, they add up in a big way.

The biggest critique I receive about this is "I can't do that!"

Of course you can. Assuming you can write with your thumbs, it's not hard at all. If you dare, you can invest in a Bluetooth keyboard, but you have to haul that around with you. Instead, just slip your phone out of your pocket and write.

Common scenarios where I've written:

- in the backseat of an Uber car
- on public transportation
- on an airplane (so I didn't have to bring my laptop)
- at the doctor's office while waiting for the doctor
- on my couch because I suffered a back injury
- standing in a long grocery checkout line
- any downtime, anywhere

Of course, don't be antisocial and don't put yourself in harm's way. But the amount of published words I've written total on my phone is unbelievable. It's helped me become insanely prolific.

Remember, your book is going to get extensively self-edited and sent to at least one editor, so it doesn't matter how you write it, as long as you do it well, cleanly, efficiently...and in one draft.

How is it possible to "get your mind in the zone" to write without an outline on your phone? After all, pantsing is hard enough on your desktop!

Practice. It doesn't happen overnight, but eventually, your brain breaks and you can pick up a story from anywhere.

I have a young child, a bunch of pets, a crazy job, and for several years, I was going to law school. That resulted in many, many days where my writing sessions were constantly interrupted. I learned how to restart my brain quickly. Sometimes, I'd only have five minutes to write for the entire day. Necessity drove me to retrain my brain so that I could continue telling a story no matter where I was, no matter when.

You can do this too if you choose.

Writing on your phone can sometimes be a *little* sloppier, but not much. Just vary your speed accordingly. I have a certain pace that I settle into that minimizes errors but maximizes my storytelling. The sections I write on my phone do not generally produce more edits than chapters I write on my desktop. I attribute this to looping (another great reason to do it regularly!)

So, consider the benefits of writing on your phone, if you dare.

If you'd like to find a good writing app for iOS or Android, use my free Writing App Database tool to find a new great app in just a few clicks at www.authorlevelup.com/writingapps.

PANTSING...WITH DICTATION???

Let's talk about yet another alternative (and maybe advanced) technique for pantsing to help you while writing your novel.

Did you also know that many writers all over the world use dictation to speak their way to higher word counts?

Did you also know that the average person types around 50 words per minute but speaks around 150? With dictation, you can more than double or triple your word count!

I won't get into the nitty-gritty of dictation because it's outside the scope of this book, but I'd like for you to consider it.

I use dictation regularly, and it has exploded my word counts along with writing on my phone.

The tools I use:

- Dragon Professional Individual (Windows). Dragon is the best dictation software out there, period. It's expensive but worth the money. Microsoft had acquired Nuance (Dragon's developer), so there may be changes in the future, but hopefully, Microsoft won't kill the app.

- A podcasting microphone. You need a good quality microphone for cleaner dictation.
- Dragon Anywhere for iOS. This is a subscription-based app that gives you decent results using your phone's microphone. You can dictate with it anywhere. I use it when I'm doing laundry or dishes. It's not as accurate as the desktop version, but it's still pretty good.

When I dictate on my desktop, I do it directly into Microsoft Word and copy and paste the finished text into my writing app.

Dictation has a learning curve, and you have to learn how to speak in a way that may feel unnatural to you. However, once you get used to it, it's like riding a bicycle. You never forget how to do it, and if you retrain your brain to pick up a story no matter the method or the place, then you'll be able to get going quickly.

Dictation is another reason I am prolific.

The only caution I'd make about dictation is that it *can* be sloppy. Take the time to learn how to do it correctly, don't go too fast, loop regularly, and follow my tips in the next chapter on editing, and your text will come out just fine.

Learning to dictate without an outline isn't easy, but once you learn it, you can exercise your true love of story by speaking it. You might even have crazy word counts to show for it. Just remember to dictate well—it's not worth the time if you have to spend an inordinate amount of time cleaning up your text. Fortunately, clean dictation is a skill that can be learned.

If you're willing to explore this topic further, I've written an entire book on how to get started with dictation—and how to apply my methods of pantsing to it. Check it out at www.authorlevelup.com/dictationbook.

AFTER YOU FINISH: PREPARING YOUR BOOK FOR PUBLICATION

THE MASTER LOOP

You're staring at a finished novel. You did it. Congratulations!

Now what?

First, take a moment and celebrate. You've accomplished something that many failed to do. Sure, writing a novel is hard, but writing one without an outline? Sheeeeeet, that puts you in the upper echelons, my friend.

The next step is to begin self-editing.

While it's true that we are writing the novel in one draft, it's a smart idea to loop through the novel one more time to catch any last-minute issues before you write "The End." I call this the master loop.

To reiterate, I'm not proposing any rewriting. This is just a rocket run through the novel to catch errors. It's not meant to be deep. If you followed the advice in this book, you will have done all the hard work. Simply fix any issues you find and move on.

I find that the best way to do a master loop is out of sequence.

If you review the novel front to back, you'll have blind spots, especially if you wrote it that way. Reviewing the chapters out of sequence will help you catch inconsistencies better.

Here's how I do it:

- Last chapter
- First chapter
- Second-to-last chapter
- Second chapter

I work my way to the exact middle of the book, which is the final chapter I review.

You would not believe how many things you catch when you review your novel this way. This is also a great way to catch issues with your villain—the villain is usually very prominent in the first and final chapters. Reviewing early and late chapters back-to-back helps bridge any issues that might exist.

Remember, I'm not advocating for rewriting. This is just a brisk run through the novel, reading for plot holes, inconsistencies, and typos. This usually takes me about a day. I'm willing to sacrifice a day because of the number of issues I find. Everything I catch is one thing my reader won't!

Enjoy your time with the master loop. Once you're done, you move back into the realm of certainty—the editorial process.

A SOLID, EASY SELF-EDITING WORKFLOW TO HELP YOU WITH CLEANER DRAFTS

Let's discuss editing.

Editing is crucial, but you already knew I was going to say that. Let's talk about my tried-and-true editing workflow that takes my novel from unedited to polished in no time.

SELF-EDITING TOOLS

You've already self-edited the book with your master loop, so the hard manual work is over. Now we just need to use some tools to help us catch issues we missed.

Microsoft Word's Editor (spelling and grammar checker) is your first port-of-call. I *only* use the spelling and grammar checks. The other checks are garbage. Use Word to catch obvious spelling and grammar errors. But remember—just because Word recommends something doesn't mean you should accept it!

My next tool is Grammarly. I use the free add-in for Microsoft Word. I've done some testing on Grammarly Premium, and my tests found it was not effective for fiction writing. Maybe that has changed, but it's still a little pricey in my opinion.

Grammarly is great. It's quite good at certain checks like comma usage, missing determiners and words, and clarity issues. That said, I don't accept everything it recommends me, just like Word. Remember, you're in charge. Don't let an app tell you how to write.

Next, I use ProWritingAid. Yes, I use *both* Grammarly and ProWritingAid. I have a lifetime license for the paid version of ProWritingAid, and that's worth the money. ProWritingAid is great at catching spelling errors that Grammarly misses, and it does a better job with policing punctuation, at least in my experience. Again, I don't use all of the tool's checks. I only use the basic ones. It serves as a helpful foil to Grammarly, though admittedly, both apps sometimes make recommendations that cancel each other out.

Next, I use PerfectIt, which is proofreading software that editors use to help them catch last-minute issues with a text, such as inconsistent spellings, word usage, and hyphenation issues. PerfectIt is not the same as Grammarly or ProWriting-Aid. It's a completely different app. I've tried to tell this to the writing community through videos on my YouTube channel, but no one will listen to me because it has a subscription, and people hate subscriptions. For this reason, PerfectIt is criminally underrated.

Another amazing benefit of PerfectIt is that it now integrates with the *Chicago Manual of Style* (CMOS), so it will run your manuscript against the *Chicago Manual of Style* and flag anything that doesn't meet a certain rule. In other words, it automates the use of the CMOS, which means you don't have to go reaching for the manual whenever you have questions about something. Few writers do this anyway, so that already makes it a win to know that you have the CMOS at your fingertips and an app is running your book against it. Very powerful.

Those are the spelling and grammar checkers I use to catch many errors. They'll help you too.

But there's more.

MICROSOFT WORD MACROS

I love Microsoft Word macros. They're underrated, and most people run away screaming when you mention them. But, wow, are they powerful.

A macro is a series of steps executed automatically by a computer. A macro saves time. For example, if you want to highlight a string of text, bold it, and then italicize it, that's tedious to do with a mouse and keyboard. Instead, you can create a macro that will do both steps with the click of a button. Most people are familiar with Microsoft Excel macros, but Word macros use the same programming language and are just as powerful.

Turns out you can create Microsoft Word macros to catch typos and grammar errors that Word's Editor, Grammarly, ProWritingAid, and PerfectIt won't catch. Think of Word macros as an added layer of protection between your spelling and grammar checkers and your editor.

Microsoft Word macros are a skill. They're not the easiest thing in the world to learn...but fortunately, you don't have to.

I wanted to use this chapter to make more people aware of Paul Beverley, who is, in my opinion, the pre-eminent world expert in Microsoft Word macros.

Paul is an editor in the United Kingdom who has created over 800 macros to assist editors in editing their clients' work.

I don't know any editors who use Word macros because, frankly, it's an acquired taste. However, Paul published a free book and dozens of videos on his website to help people understand why they are important. He also does training sessions. His macros are free.

While Paul's target audience is editors, there's no reason *writers* can't use his macros.

When I first discovered Paul's work a few years ago, I will admit that I couldn't "see" how macros could help me. I didn't even know what a macro was at the time.

It took a few years for things to "click," and now that they have, I believe that Paul is an underrated gift to the writing community.

Here are a few of his macros:

- ProperNounAlyse produces a list of all the proper nouns in your story so you can tell if anything is accidentally misspelled.
- HyphenAlyse scans your story for any words that should be hyphenated.
- Comments Exporter exports all of your editor's comments to a table so you can review them all together.
- Tracked Changes counter counts the number of tracked changes you receive from your editor.

And more. Around 800 more, to be exact.

But perhaps the most powerful tool Paul created is a macro called FREdit.

FREdit is a scripted find and replace. Let's illustrate its usefulness with a common problem that Scrivener users have.

For some reason, Scrivener doesn't handle curly quotes consistently. Sometimes it puts the quotes facing the wrong way —especially if you use quotes after an em dash. It's maddening.

If you wanted to eliminate this problem manually, you could search for an em dash followed by an open quote, replace all with an em dash followed by a close quote.

Or you could load these characters into FREdit and it will catch them every time, along with any other error you want to catch.

Maybe your next book won't have the weird em dash issue. FREdit will simply skip it as if it didn't exist and move on to the next issue.

So FREdit acts as a database for your errors and flags them any time they show up in your writing.

I hope you can see now why this is so powerful, and why it is now an indispensable part of my workflow.

We have Paul Beverley to thank for his macro brilliance.

Check out his website at http://www.archivepub.co.uk.

I use around a dozen of Paul's macros to help me catch additional errors.

Most importantly, I feed edits that my editors make into FREdit so that I won't make the same mistake again. For example, I used the word "cadence" incorrectly in a sentence. FREdit will highlight the word any time I use it in the future, ensuring correct usage.

The great thing about FREdit is that you're teaching it errors your editor has caught in the past. Over time, it can help you generate cleaner manuscripts.

Finally, Paul's macros are great, but I also have some of my own. I hired a programmer on Fiverr to create a handful of macros for me. I paid around $200 for all of them. The most prominent of these is my repeated word macro. It highlights all words that are repeated within a certain radius. (ProWritingAid offers this too, but I like the functionality of my macro better.) This macro is useful for me because I tend to repeat words without realizing it.

I did all of this without learning a single line of code. I just watched a few YouTube videos and then I was catching extra errors in my work.

Take a look at Microsoft Word macros. They'll surprise you. And they'll help you achieve the goal of writing cleanly.

FACT-CHECKERS

Let's return to the efficiency problem. There's one element of the manuscript that we did not resolve. If we don't do anything about it, then we may have dissatisfied readers.

Can you guess what the problem is? Our research!

Before we started writing, we practiced foundational research and that gave us a good start to the story. As we wrote the story, we practiced just-in-time research, which also helped us save time and effort by researching only what needed to be included in the story.

How do you know if your research is accurate? In other words, if you write that a historical event happened because of X, how do you know that your research was correct, and it wasn't Y instead? What if you write about a legal procedure in the courtroom, but it's wrong?

That's where fact-checkers come in. They check the *execution* of your research. I've never heard anyone talk about this, so I'm in my own galaxy...but hear me out.

You can do all of the research in the world for your novel, but if you make mistakes or rely on inaccurate information, it will put readers off. So

we must think of *research* not as something we do before and while we're writing, but also as a function of *editing*.

To solve this problem, you hire people to check your research. They're called fact-checkers.

Who are these people and where do you find them? They are not editors and they are not readers. They're regular people who happen to have the experience you're looking for.

I choose two or three subject areas in the novel that are important to the story, and then I look for fact-checkers. I only choose subjects that have a material impact on the plot and characters.

You can look locally for a fact-checker or you can find them online. I've had the best luck with Upwork, which is a site where you hire freelancers.

You don't send fact-checkers the entire book. You only send them the sections that need to be checked.

For example, in my *Chicago Rat Shifter* series, the story takes place in Chicago. I have been to Chicago many times for work and pleasure, but I have never lived there. I recruited two Chicago natives to read the Chicago scenes to let me know if anything was factually wrong.

As another example with the same series, the main character is a rat shifter. I didn't know very much about rats. I did some solid foundational and just-in-time research, but I thought it would be smart to find someone who specialized in rodent biology to read my rat scenes to help me make them more realistic. I found a biologist who spent a lot of time with rats to help me. I only sent him the scenes where the main character shifted into a rat.

Just seeing how fact-checkers *think* is worth it. One of my Chicago fact-checkers made an off-hand comment that ended up in the manuscript and made a particular section pop. Their feedback is extremely valuable.

Fact-checkers help you validate whether the research you did was correct. That's why I believe you need to think of research as a function of editing. Fact-checkers are especially important when you are writing what you don't know.

Fact-checkers serve the goal of helping you write well, cleanly, and efficiently. They help you write well because their feedback will strengthen the manuscript. They help you write cleanly because they can catch typos if you want them to. And they help you write efficiently (with the next book) because if your next book is in the same series, then you can apply their feedback to the next story, which means less foundational research but a more well-written story.

I know you still may have questions about this. Read below for more details of my story of how I hired fact-checkers for my *Chicago Rat Shifter* series.

―――

So much in life boils down to picking the right people.

In the writing life, this means hiring the right editor and cover designer. "Right" is subjective, but for me, the right person does what they say they are going to do when they say they are going to do it, gives you a quality product that indicates they treated your work with care, and they offer a drama-free experience. I have zero patience for drama.

For my latest novel, I hired fact-checkers to assist me in validating the research for my book. I needed to fill six positions and posted them on Upwork. Within hours, I had dozens of proposals, far more people than I could hire!

As a former hiring manager at work who was responsible for hiring and firing people, with a pretty good track record of hiring good talent, I am methodical and ruthless in my hiring process. I weed out candidates quickly.

I had three jobs:

- two fact-checkers to review the Chicago scenes in my story
- two fact-checkers to review the rodent biology in the story (the novel features rats prominently)
- two female readers to read chapters with the hero's sister to verify how well the female readers will respond to her

Here are my criteria for any job:

1. Does the person have the skills to do the job?
2. Does the person have the will to do the job? In other words, what signals show me that they want it?
3. Are there any red flags?

For the Chicago fact-checkers, I had two requirements:

- The person needs to either live in Chicago or have lived there for a long time, preferably with knowledge of the Logan Square neighborhood.
- They had to describe their Chicago background.

Without exception, almost all of the applicants were Chicagoans or people who lived there for at least five years or more.

As I reviewed their proposals about their qualifications and why they wanted the job, I paid careful attention to:

- Red flags in their responses. I looked for anything

that seemed odd. On a platform like Upwork, sometimes people will say anything to get a job. Sometimes they even post stock language to every proposal. Those people always receive hard no's from me. Once you weed those people out, you usually have a lot of good people left.

- Their enthusiasm. A lot of freelancers found the job intriguing and unusual compared to their usual gigs. One freelancer even offered to visit locations in person and take photos and videos of the areas so that I could make the writing even more realistic. I like to reward genuine enthusiasm.
- Their track records on the platform. Anyone with a history of bad performance received additional scrutiny. Is the bad performance something they did or did they catch a bad break with a crazy client? There are lots of crazy clients out there—I know that first-hand, so I have some sympathy. First-time freelancers were acceptable.

Ultimately, I selected a Chicago native who lived on the South Side his entire life and a Northwest-sider who lived in Logan Square for a long time. Both met the deadline, offered detailed feedback, and gave me exactly what I needed. No hassles and no drama.

My rodent biology job was tougher. I needed someone who had a biology degree or who had extensive experience working with rats.

I received proposals from people on the platform who were qualified—a fair number of doctors and seasoned biologists. One candidate worked in pest control. However, the struggle was finding someone who I thought could convey biological details to me in a format I could understand, and who would give me information that I could use in the story. There was also a language barrier with some candidates. I only hired one person who met my criteria, and he was one of the more unusual candidates who, on paper, didn't meet my criteria. He didn't have a biology degree. He went to school for biology and worked with rats for a long time, but he decided he wanted to do something different with his career. He did editing on the side. He ended up being the perfect candidate because he gave me scientific details but in a format I could use.

I found the other rodent fact-checker elsewhere. I prefer not to settle when hiring people. Settling always leads to trouble.

The female beta readers also went smoothly. I was looking for:

- a female who had a younger brother
- someone who could give me feedback on whether the female character in my story was believable or not.

I ultimately selected two candidates who told me stories about their relationship with their brother that were most like the relationship in my novel. One delivered good, detailed feedback. The other ghosted me after I hired her, so that was a pain. I hired my third choice, who delivered good feedback in a couple of days.

Sometimes you hire bad fits. Sometimes you should have seen the red flags earlier; other times, there's no way you could have known the person would be a bad fit. That's what happens when you engage with so many random people. Sometimes you pick 'em wrong. That's just how it goes.

But when you pick the right people for projects, it makes the projects go smoother. You also do a service to your readers because you make their reading experience more enjoyable.

My final point with fact-checkers is to reiterate that you want to pick two or three subject areas in your story that you lack expertise in. These subjects should be important to the story, and, if you got them wrong, they would result in bad reviews. That's how you determine what needs to be checked.

Your story may not have any of these subjects, and if so, that's okay. My experience is that most stories have at least one, though.

Fact-checkers will help you flesh out your story in a very real way that will have a direct impact with readers.

BETA READERS

Here's everything you ever wanted to know about beta readers.

What are beta readers?

Beta readers are volunteers who agree to read your book and offer feedback.

Beta reading happens when you feel like you've done as much self-editing as you possibly can. You then send it to beta readers for feedback.

Beta readers offer you their comments, observations, and suggestions for improvement of your manuscript before publication, *before* sending it to your professional editor.

Ideal beta readers can be trusted authors, recruited readers, family, or friends. The first qualification is that they are well-read in your genre (not much point in giving your young adult lesbian mermaid romance to a space opera fan) and the second qualification is that they'll give you an honest assessment.

In my personal opinion (and experience), the best beta reader is someone who is *not* a family member or a friend. Bless your family and friends, but they don't have the objectivity that you need.

Should I use beta readers?

That's up to you. Some authors swear by them, others prefer to work alone until they pass the work to a professional editor. The best way to find out is to try it.

What should I look for in a beta reader?

Honesty, above all. Don't recruit anyone who will be overly nice and positive for fear of hurting your feelings. This isn't about self-aggrandizement or creating an echo chamber—it's about honest feedback.

You want articulate people who can convey what they think clearly, but who aren't prescriptive. A beta reader who claims that all the major characters have to be introduced in the first chapter, or that a chapter should always begin with a summary of what happened in the last, is an opinionated person who is fonder of their own theories than of your book.

You also want to focus on developmental, structural, or substantive editing. You're looking for feedback about big issues —plot, character, pacing, and voice in fiction; argument, structure, and voice in nonfiction—not detailed issues of word choice or sentence structure.

How many beta readers do I need?

Three is the magic number, but I wouldn't do more than five. The wider the range of opinions you receive, the better, so think about the quality and mix, as well as the number of your beta readers.

Where do I find beta readers?

You can search online for "find beta readers" and see what comes up. Increasingly, some readers offer paid beta reader services. There are also Facebook and Goodreads for beta reader groups, but make sure to read the group rules and follow them to the letter. You can also reach out to author friends.

Treat your beta readers well and remember: they're volunteering their time to help you. Expect delays, and expect some readers not to follow through with their promise. Having a couple of betas will insulate you against this risk.

Should I use beta readers?

It depends on your story. I rarely use them, but they do have their benefits. I'll typically use them when I'm venturing into a new genre. Otherwise, I skip this step and move to a copyeditor.

Should I pay beta readers?

In my experience, a paid beta reader meets their deadlines and gives you better feedback. They're regular people who have lives. Your book is not their first priority, but they'll adjust if you compensate them for their time.

WORKING WITH EDITORS

The two types of editors I use are copyeditors and proofreaders. I don't use developmental editors because developmental edits are against the philosophy of this method—these types of editors often recommend structural edits and substantial rewrites, which I just don't believe in. So I'm not covering them in this book.

Copyeditors make your novel feel like a finished novel. They'll review the book line by line and make spelling and grammar corrections, ensure that the words on the page are the right words, and also catch any glaring plot holes. However, don't rely on a copyeditor to help you with story. That's not why you hire them. Use beta readers instead.

Proofreaders check your copyeditor's work in addition to any remaining pesky formatting issues with the text. I highly recommend proofreaders.

This book isn't intended to be a guide to finding an editor. You can read my book *150 Self-Publishing Questions Answered* for a comprehensive guide to finding and working with an editor.

After you've sent the book to a copyeditor and a proofreader, it's ready for publication.

But there are a few more things you can do before proceeding. Keep reading to venture into the rabbit hole...

INTO THE RABBIT HOLE: MINING YOUR STORIES FOR DATA & ANALYTICS TO HELP YOU WRITE THE NEXT BOOK BETTER

Warning: this chapter is optional and advanced. Don't feel like you have to follow it. I have used the techniques in this chapter to cut down on spelling and grammar errors in my work, and to collaborate with my editors more effectively.

Before we proceed, let me make a critical point: a writer who doesn't know how to tame their critical voice will read this section and conclude all the wrong things from it. I hesitated to include this chapter because my greatest fear is that people will read it and let their critical voices take over.

Do not let any of what you are about to read into your writing process. Ever. This information is solely to be used while editing. If you can't manage your critical voice, then this chapter will work against you. Don't read it.

However, I ultimately decided to include it because I want to show people what the next levels of writing look like when you can tame your critical voice. The few who have the ears to hear the message in this chapter can use the information to do tremendous good in their writing.

Once you receive your book back from your editor, you can simply review the edits and then proceed to formatting and publication, but you're missing an opportunity: analyzing your writing.

When people think of "analyzing their writing," they think of apps that give them useless data like the number of times they use an adverb, word frequency distributions, or statistics about their word counts. I'm not talking about those.

I'm talking about deeper, fundamental questions that you can answer on your own with a little elbow grease. How did you *do* with your writing? How many edits did your editor suggest? How many story issues did they catch?

I'll share a process that I follow to glean important insights from my editor's edits. I'll tell you how I do it, and if this resonates with you, it'll be up to you to figure out the rest from here.

TURNING MY EDITS INTO DATA

When I receive a book from my editor, I use Paul Beverley's Tracked Changes Counter macro to count the total number of tracked changes and comments.

View in high resolution at
www.authorlevelup.com/pantsingimages

    I'm only interested in the number of edits. Comments are useful to analyze to see how many of them are story related versus spelling and grammar, but that's another rabbit hole that I'm not going to go into to keep this chapter simple.

    The numbers Tracked Changes Counter gives you are not true number of edits. When your editor deletes something and inserts a replacement, that counts as two edits, so the number of edits contains duplicates. As a general rule, I divide the tracked changes number by half to get the true number of edits.

Let's say I receive 563 edits, but that's 282 edits if I divide it in half. The novel is 60,000 words. If we do some more math and divide the total word count of the manuscript by the number of edits, that means that I received one edit per 212 words. Are you with me so far?

$563 \text{ words} / 2 = 282 \text{ edits}$

$60,000 \text{ words} / 282 \text{ edits} = 1 \text{ edit per } 212 \text{ words}$

View in high resolution at
www.authorlevelup.com/pantsingimages

We could do some additional analysis to create a full set of benchmarks:

- 282 edits
- 1 edit per 212 words (or, 1 edit per 1.5 pages)

The next questions to ask are, "what were the biggest drivers of my edits" and "how can I improve my edits per?" (The higher, the better).

The best way to discover the answers is to look at your edits. However, scrolling through and reading them one by one is not efficient or helpful. Instead, use Microsoft Word's outline feature to cut your chapters into single Word documents.

View in high resolution at
www.authorlevelup.com/pantsingimages

Then, you have three choices: go into each document and

use the Tracked Changes Counter on each one (easiest, but time-consuming), hire someone to do this for you, or hire a programmer on Fiverr to create a macro that reads each file and outputs the number of tracked changes (and comments) on a spreadsheet.

Whether you do this step manually or programmatically, you want to create a document that contains the chapter, number of changes, and number of comments.

View in high resolution at
www.authorlevelup.com/pantsingimages

(I won't share my spreadsheet template because it's a little finicky and I don't have the time to troubleshoot for folks. Sorry. But this is something you can hire someone to do for you. The way the sheet works is that you choose a folder where your Word docs are located and then the macro does the rest. I paid less than $50 for this.)

Throw those numbers into another Excel spreadsheet. Or, if you really wanted to do some deeper analysis, put them into your advanced reverse outline. (See why I love Excel so much?)

Sort your chapters. Which ones received the most edits? Pick your top three offenders and scroll through the edits for those chapters. If you see a certain type of error more than once, write it down because you might be able to feed it into FREdit.

What are the commonalities in the mistakes you're making? You might not find any, but I sure did.

(Keep in mind that what I'm discussing below are edits related to spelling and grammar, not story. You can't effectively do this kind of analysis with story.)

When I dug into my data, it turned out that my highest edited chapters had several indicators in common:

- chapters I wrote while in "flow"
- chapters greater than 2,500 words
- chapters where I introduced a new character
- the presence of writer's block in a chapter (i.e., chapters with stormy sky visibility)

I am NOT saying that these will be indicators of edits for your work. I am only sharing the findings from my work. If you use these assumptions without validating them, you will hurt your editing efforts.

Let's go through the indicators.

Flow. At first glance, it seems counterintuitive that chapters written in flow would produce more errors, but it makes sense if you think about it. This is because when I enter flow, I stop thinking about typing. I'm only thinking about the story. So I make more mistakes. My data bore that out. I've written a lot of novels into the dark, so I have more data than the average person.

Chapters greater than 2,500 words. My data consistently showed that chapters greater than 2,500 words produced more edits than chapters with lower word counts. This makes sense because the more words you have in a chapter, the more chances you have for errors.

Chapters where I introduce a major new character. This observation was interesting because the edits aren't (necessarily) in the character details, which is where you might expect them. The introduction of a new character is just an indicator that I am more likely to have a higher number of edits in a chapter. I can't explain this one, but again, the data suggests a correlation with regular frequency.

Chapters with stormy sky visibility. I always like to mark the chapters with rough spots because a rough spot directly correlates with a higher number of edits. This is also difficult to explain, but it could be because when I'm microfocusing, I'm also not paying attention to typing. I'm so preoccupied with getting the story down that I don't see typos as much probably.

The creepy thing about these indicators is that once I discovered them, they *predicted* which chapters in my subsequent books would have the highest number of edits. Not once, not twice, but multiple times, with stunning accuracy. I even shared this with a data analyst in my community who validated my hypotheses.

The next question is, "What do I do with this data?"

There are a few things you can do. First, you can see which edits are programmable into a macro like FREdit to help you eliminate them, therefore reducing your edits over time. Second, you can see which edits are easy things you can remember so you can minimize them next time. Third, you can use this data to tell you which chapters to spend more time on during your master loop. Fourth, you can use this data to flag potential problem chapters for your editor so they can spend more time on them.

I can go much deeper into this topic, but I hope this at least shows you a different way of thinking about your editing. I call it "editing analytics"—using data and analytics of your own work to help you improve the quality of your manuscript.

I share my findings with you to challenge you to think about your words as data. *My* data shouldn't matter to you—it's useful only to me. What matters is what you discover in your own work.

As for me, I have dramatically reduced the number of edits in my manuscripts. By the time I hand over my novels to my editor, my manuscripts are moderately clean. My benchmarks are 275 edits per novel on average (across copyediting and proofreading) and one edit per 200 words (which is approximately 1 edit per 1.5 pages with Times New Roman, size 12 font, double-spaced). Per all the editors I've worked with, that's clean, but I want to do better. Combined with good editors and the safeguards I've discussed previously around character, story, and setting details, I'm giving my novel the best possible shot of connecting with readers. In the words of famed football coach Art Williams, "All you can do is all you can do, and all you can do is enough!" I want to make sure I'm doing all I can do—while writing well, cleanly, efficiently, and in one draft, of course!

Your benchmark numbers might be better or worse than mine, but we're not in competition with each other. The best person to compete against is yourself. Figure out your benchmarks and learn how to beat them.

What are YOUR benchmarks? Can you learn to think about your books as data so that you can find ways to improve your writing?

This path isn't for everyone, and it's not for the faint of heart. But maybe this chapter will give you some ideas on how you can glean lessons from your editor, lessons that you can use.

If you like this chapter, I've written an entire (advanced)

book on this topic called The Author Editing Problem. It goes deep into my editing process, Microsoft Word macros, and more. Check it out at www.authorlevelup.com/editing.

PARTING WORDS

Pantsing is a wonderful way to write. It connects you with your creative voice, and your creative voice will take you amazing places if you have the courage to listen.

You'll do well on your journey if you remember a few things.

- Always aim to write well, cleanly, and efficiently, no matter what.
- Avoid rewriting. Your critical voice will kill your stories.
- Keep a positive mindset and manage your emotions.
- Keep learning the craft and committing to being a better writer.
- Practice foundational research and just-in-time research, and validate your research in editing with fact-checkers. This will help you write better stories.
- Remember the different areas of the novel as you're writing and employ the strategies in this book to deal with rough spots. Consistency + curiosity + tenacity = success.

- Be ruthless but efficient while editing your book. Be known for sending clean manuscripts to your editor. But better yet, be known for generating clean manuscripts quickly. The cleaner your manuscript is, the better!
- (Optional) Consider the power of your words as data, and harness that data to help you make targeted, data-based decisions to improve the quality of your manuscript before sending it to an editor.

I love the entire process of writing: learning, writing, business, marketing, and everything in between. But more than anything, I love the thrill of sitting at my computer without any clue of what I'm going to write and producing a finished manuscript. It never gets old. Every novel is different and each one teaches me something about the craft, and more importantly, a life lesson.

Anything in life is possible if you have courage. This is true with your writing too.

Happy writing, happy pantsing, and good luck out there. I've taught you everything I know about pantsing. Now go write!

RESOURCES MENTIONED IN THIS BOOK

The following resources were mentioned in this book:

Books on Outlining

Writing into the Dark by Dean Wesley Smith
Story Trumps Structure by Steve James

Books on Plotting

Screenplay by Syd Field
Story Engineering by Larry Brooks

High-Resolution Images in This Book

View them at www.authorlevelup.com/pantsingimages.

Helpful Videos

In addition to these, check out a video playlist on my YouTube channel on how to create engaging characters: www.authorlevelup.com/engagingcharacters.

READ NEXT: HOW TO DICTATE
A BOOK

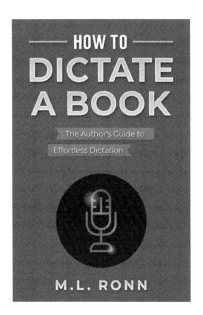

Have you heard that dictation supercharges your word counts, but are you frustrated with it?

You're not alone. Many writers attempt dictation, only to

quit because it doesn't get them the results they hear so much about. Fortunately, there is a way to do it correctly.

If you've ever worried about "sounding funny", struggled with what to say when you're behind the mic, or gotten tired of making a kajillion spelling mistakes with Dragon, then you've come to the right place.

In this writer's guide, prolific author M.L. Ronn will teach you how to unlock the power of dictation using the methods he's used to dictate over 30 books of fiction & nonfiction.

You'll learn:

- How to dictate (and why you should)
- The tools and equipment you'll need
- How to set Dragon up for success
- The 3 types of dictation (the 2nd one will blow your mind)
- How to dictate cleanly the first time so that you don't have to spend as much time editing
- * And more

This book also comes with a complimentary video companion course where you can see the author dictate sections from this very book. Watch along as you read or watch the course first and then return to the text for more nuance. (No email address required. Just click and enjoy).

If you're ready to become a dictation master, then click the buy button and speak your way to writing nirvana!

Get your copy today at www.authorlevelup.com/dictationbook.

MEET M.L. RONN

Science fiction and fantasy on the wild side!

M.L. Ronn (Michael La Ronn) is the author of many science fiction and fantasy novels including *The Good Necromancer, Android X,* and *The Last Dragon Lord* series.

In 2012, a life-threatening illness made him realize that storytelling was his #1 passion. He's devoted his life to writing ever since, making up whatever story makes him fall out of his chair laughing the hardest. Every day.

Learn more about Michael
www.authorlevelup.com (for writers)
www.michaellaronn.com (fiction)

Interactive Fiction: How to Engage Readers and Push the Boundaries of Story Telling
Indie Poet Rock Star
Indie Poet Formatting
2016 Indie Author State of the Union

More Books for Writers:

www.authorlevelup.com/books

Fiction:
www.michaellaronn.com/books

Made in United States
Troutdale, OR
01/16/2024

16968663R00135